Delicious
Poke Cakes

Delicious Poke Cakes

Roxanne Wyss & Kathy Moore

Photographs by Staci Valentine

ST. MARTIN'S GRIFFIN
NEW YORK

www.stmartins.com

Book design: Rita Sowins / Sowins Design
Food stylist: Alyse Sakai

The Library of Congress Cataloging-in-Publication Data is available upon request.

ISBN 978-1-250-13584-1 (trade paperback)
ISBN 978-1-250-13585-8 (ebook)

Our books may be purchased in bulk for promotional, educational, or business use. Please contact your local bookseller or the Macmillian Corporate and Premium Sales Department at 1-800-221-7945, extension 5442, or by email at MacmillianSpecialMarkets@macmillian.com.

First Edition: November 2017

10 9 8 7 6 5 4 3 2 1

We dedicate this book to
our families—Roxanne's family,
Bob and Grace Bateman,
and Kathy's family, David, Laura,
and Amanda Moore—
whose love makes our lives sweeter.

Contents

Introduction

Put an end to dry, tasteless cakes and quickly transform a ho-hum cake into something glorious. Just poke, pour, and enjoy! The recipes in *Delicious Poke Cakes* make it easy.

Begin with a baked cake, prepared from a box mix or by following one of the simple from-scratch cake recipes included here. Poke holes in the cake with a fork, the handle of a wooden spoon, a straw, or a skewer. Pour a pudding, topping, glaze, gelatin, or sauce over the cake and let the flavor seep into every crevice and permeate every morsel of cake, soaking the cake with all the goodness and flavor. Finish it off with a luscious frosting or topping, and now that everyday cake has pizzazz. You will discover a wonderful flavor boost in every bite.

The unsurpassed make-ahead convenience of these cakes means they are year-round winners for busy cooks. Poke cakes are perfect for everyday family dinners, for all those special holiday celebrations, and for every delicious gathering all year long. Some believe the first poke cake may have been a white cake drizzled with colorful gelatin and frosted with whipped topping. On the other hand, old-fashioned pound cakes were often poked with a fork and drizzled with juice. Both are great, but this recipe collection doesn't stop there. There is a recipe for every taste—decadent chocolates and caramels, fresh fruit, and more. Serve a fun, updated classic cake; a colorful kid-friendly dessert; or an adults-only cake laced with liquor.

With all these enticing flavors, don't forget that effortless, no-fuss cooking is the real treat. The ingredients are basic and may be waiting in your pantry already.
Never again shy away from making dessert, and rest assured that your cake will be the hit of the party, potluck, or picnic. No stress—just rave reviews.

Just bake the cake, poke, pour, and serve.

Poke Cake
Basics

EASY

1. **Bake a cake.** Many are baked in a 9 x 13-inch pan, but some of the recipes are for layer cakes, loaf cakes, or Bundt cakes. Spray the pan with nonstick cooking spray. Use the size of the pan recommended in the recipe. After baking, leave the cake in the pan, unless otherwise directed in the recipe.

2. **Poke the cake.** The recipes will tell you what to poke the cake with and when to poke it. Sometimes you poke the cake soon after taking it out of the oven; sometimes the cake needs to cool completely.

WHAT TO USE TO POKE THE CAKE?

Fine holes	A fork is great for making lots of fine holes. Use it when pouring liquids over a cake.
Small holes	A round-ended skewer makes a small hole about 1/16 inch in diameter.
Medium holes	A drinking straw makes medium-size holes about 1/4 inch in diameter.
Large holes	The rounded end on the handle of a wooden spoon, about 1/2 inch in diameter, is perfect for making larger holes for thicker sauces or toppings.

Use larger holes for thicker or chunky toppings and smaller holes for liquids. Follow the recommendation in the recipe.

Poke holes evenly over the entire surface of the cake. The more holes, the better, especially when poking with a fork.

Poke the holes deep into the cake, but do not punch through the bottom of the cake—you don't want the flavorful liquid to seep out.

3. **Pour the topping or sauce over the cake.** Pour the syrup, topping, or sauce very slowly, drizzling it over every spot on the cake and filling the holes. Sometimes you will

want to stop and let the liquid seep into the cake, then pour some more. Sometimes you may want to use the back of a spoon or the tip of a table knife to help spread the sauce and fill the holes.

If the liquid seems to pool in one particular spot, you may find you want to poke a hole in that very spot.

4. Frost the cake. There is a suggestion on each recipe, such as whipped topping, whipped cream, or luscious frosting. We offer a really tasty suggestion that is our favorite, but of course, you can select another frosting if that is your preference.

TIPS FOR THE BEST RESULTS

❋ Which pan? A 9 x 13-inch baking dish is often used for these recipes. Metal and glass both work for these recipes, but we often choose a glass baking dish, as it is attractive for serving. Occasionally, we use 9-inch round cake pans, loaf pans, and Bundt pans. Use the size of pan recommended in the recipe.

❋ Spray the pan with nonstick cooking spray. For a Bundt cake, we find that nonstick baking spray with flour works well.

❋ Bake the cake for the recommended time and test for doneness. Often that means inserting a wooden pick into the center of the cake; the cake is done if the pick comes out clean. Other tests for doneness include checking to see if the sides of the cake begin to pull away from the sides of the pan or gently pressing the top to see if it springs back. Carefully test the cake, and if it's not done, return it to the oven to bake for 2 or 3 minutes more, then test it again. Repeat until the cake is done. Use hot pad holders and be cautious, as the cake and oven are hot.

❋ Leave 9 x 13-inch cakes in the pan. Poke cakes baked in a 9 x 13-inch pan are left in the pan so all of the topping you poke and pour over the cake permeates the cake.

Cakes baked in layer cake pans and Bundt pans are removed from the pan. Be sure to follow the recipe as to when to remove the cake from the pan.

For Bundt cakes, you will sometimes poke the surface of the baked cake and pour a flavorful sauce over it, then invert it, poke more holes, and pour more sauce over it. Talk about a lot of flavor! When we do this, we recommend inverting the cake onto a wire rack placed over a foil-lined rimmed baking sheet. This will ensure that the bottom of the cake does not become soggy from sitting in the glaze. To easily move the cake from the rack to a cake plate, use two long pancake turners and carefully lift the cake.

* If the poke portion has gelatin in it, stir the gelatin in boiling water until it is completely dissolved. If that topping is made with a pudding mix, mix the pudding with milk until it is completely blended. Pour the dissolved gelatin or blended pudding over the poked holes in the cake immediately after stirring and before the gelatin or pudding thicken. The recipes were tested with regular gelatin or instant pudding; sugar-free pudding or gelatin is not recommended.

* Refrigerate? Many of the cakes need to be refrigerated once the flavorful sauce or topping is poured over the top. This is especially true if it is poked and poured with gelatin, pudding, or other toppings that must set up before adding the frosting.

Cover the top of the cake with plastic wrap, then refrigerate the cake. Follow the instruction in each recipe.

Cakes with gelatin, pudding, whipped topping, whipped cream, or cream cheese frosting need to be stored in the refrigerator.

* Make-ahead convenience. Read the recipe and plan ahead. Many of the cakes are best prepared the day before.

BASIC INGREDIENTS FOR POKE CAKES

Accurately measuring the ingredients is always the first step toward the best baking result. Baking is a precise science, so measure carefully.

Follow the recipes, using the ingredients listed. Substituting other ingredients, especially those that are labeled "lower fat" or "light" or those that are formulated for special diets or to avoid specific allergens may affect the results.

{ Butter } Choose unsalted (sweet) butter.

❊ **Soften:** Butter is softened when the butter holds its shape when pressed lightly with a fingertip, but a slight indentation remains. You can set the butter out of the refrigerator for a few minutes, but softened butter is best a little colder (ideally between 65°F and 70°F) than typical kitchens in the United States. If time is short and you forgot to set it out of the refrigerator, you can quickly soften the butter by cutting it into pieces and placing them on a microwave-safe glass plate. Microwave on Medium-Low (20%) power for 10 to 15 seconds for 4 tablespoons (½ stick) butter or 20 to 25 seconds for ½ cup (1 stick) butter, until it just starts to soften. Let the butter stand for 10 minutes, then proceed with the recipe. Do not melt the butter unless the recipe specifies melted butter.

We buy butter whenever we see it on sale. It can be frozen for up to 6 months.

Low-fat, light, soft, whipped, or tub-style butter all have a different formulation than sticks of butter and are not recommend for these recipes, as the texture and the flavor of the baked cake will be adversely affected.

For optimum flavor, we generally do not recommend using margarine. One exception to this is when making Easy Decorator's Frosting (see page 116).

{ Cake Mix }

Many poke cake recipes begin with a cake mix.

Cake mixes are available in both double- and single-layer-size packages. Cake mixes sized to make double-layer cakes are commonly used for poke cakes. Follow the recipe recommendation for the best results.

The package weight for many double-layer cake mixes ranges from 15.25 to 18 ounces, especially for common flavors such as yellow, chocolate, and vanilla cake. The national brands, including Betty Crocker, Pillsbury, and Duncan Hines, and many of the store brands generally seem to fall within this range. This is the weight range we used for testing these recipes. Some specific flavors range in weight from 16 to 19 ounces. When selecting a cake mix, we recommend using one of approximately the same weight as listed in the recipe. The exact weight of the mix varies with the brand and the flavor, and we have found that slight deviations do not affect the outcome.

Cake mixes with pudding in the mix (often labeled "extra moist") and those without pudding work equally well. Use either type of cake mix for the poke cake recipes in this book. If the poke cake recipe you are using recommends beating the cake mix with a pudding mix, and your cake mix lists that it has pudding in it, go ahead and include the separate package of pudding mix just as the recipe recommends.

Can you interchange flavors? Sure, but we recommend you choose a similar flavor for the best results. For example, if the recipe lists devil's food cake and you choose to use a chocolate cake mix, the poke cake recipe will work fine. Similarly, yellow cake mix and white cake mix can be interchanged with good results.

You will spot several brands of cake mix on the grocery store shelf; experiment a little to determine which you enjoy the most.

Stock up on the cake mixes when they are on sale. Be sure to double check the date code and use the cake mixes before they expire.

See page 10 to make your own cake—without using a mix.

For some cakes, we begin the recipe with a cake mix and then list eggs, water, and oil as directed on the cake mix box. Go ahead and make the cake following the package directions. For others, we started with a cake mix and added flavor with such additions as buttermilk, sour cream, fruit juice, or other ingredients. They are very tasty—but you are always welcome to prepare the cake just as the box recommends without the flavor enhancements.

Gluten-free cake mixes can be used. Prepare the mixes as directed, then follow the poke cake recipe for the toppings or poke-and-pour portions. Many gluten-free cake mixes are designed to make one (8-or 9-inch) layer cake, so to make a 9 x 13-inch cake, make two boxes of cake mix and double all the ingredients listed on the box. The baking time may have to be extended by about 5 minutes for the larger cake; the cake is done when a wooden pick inserted into the center comes out clean. For specific information on baking with a gluten-free mix, contact the company. You may want to experiment with various brands to find the ones you prefer. Be sure the other ingredients for the poke cake are also gluten free. (See the variation on page 11 for a gluten-free yellow cake.)

{ Eggs }

The recipes were tested using large eggs. Results will not be consistent if you use medium or jumbo eggs or egg substitutes.

{ Milk and Other Liquids: }

Milk is often used in the recipes, and for optimum flavor, use regular whole dairy milk. In a pinch, 2% or reduced-fat milk can be used.

We love the tang of buttermilk. If you don't have buttermilk on hand, pour 1 tablespoon distilled white vinegar or lemon juice into a 1-cup measure and add milk to equal 1 cup. Allow it to stand for a few minutes, then measure out the volume you need for the recipe you are preparing.

{ Oil }

For baking, choose flavorless "neutral" oils, like canola, corn, or vegetable oil, and save those oils with a distinctive flavor like olive oil or walnut oil for other cooking tasks.

{ Pecans, Walnuts, and Other Nuts }

Toasting pecans, walnuts, almonds, or other nuts intensifies their flavor. To toast nuts, spread them out in a single layer on a rimmed baking sheet. Toast in a preheated 350°F for 5 to 7 minutes or until lightly toasted.

{ Whipped Topping or Whipped Cream }

Which do you prefer? We use both and if used as the frosting on top of a cake, the choice is up to you. One (8-ounce) tub frozen whipped topping, thawed, equals a little more than 3 cups. To achieve about that same volume, To substitute whipped cream and achieve about that same volume, whip 1½ cups of heavy cream until stiff peaks form.

    To whip heavy cream, chill a large, deep bowl in the freezer along with the beaters for your mixer (chilling the bowl and beaters helps the cream stiffen more quickly). Pour the cream into the chilled bowl. To keep splatters to a minimum, using a handheld mixer, begin beating on low speed, then gradually increase the speed to medium-high. Gradually beat in about 2 tablespoons confectioners' sugar per cup of cream, or sweeten to taste and beat until the cream holds stiff peaks, meaning the cream will hold its shape when you lift the beaters out of the bowl.

EQUIPMENT TO USE FOR POKE CAKES

* **Wire rack:** Most of the recipes recommend setting the cake on a wire rack to cool.

* **Mixer:** The recipes work well with a handheld mixer—no need to get out the big stand mixer.

Make Your Own Cakes

We grew up in the suburbs of Kansas City, and yes, our moms participated in the cake-mix frenzy of that time. Roxanne's mom was a busy working mom and loved to tease her dad that the cake she was serving was from scratch. That is, she would exclaim, "I scratched the label off the box!" Make no mistake, she was a great baker from scratch but as her working demands and the busy schedule of raising children became jam-packed, cake mixes were part of her repertoire.

Kathy's mom was also a busy working mom and the time crunch interrupted her scratch baking. For birthdays and holidays she often used those old family recipes, but cake mixes were favored for everyday dinners. All of those desserts she took to the church potluck dinners and the refreshments for scout meetings were lovingly made with cake mixes. Then she took a cake-decorating class and cake mixes saved the day, for she made a decorated cake each week—just for practice.

So, there is a time and place for mixes! While baking mixes first came on the market during the Depression, companies you still recognize today, including Pillsbury, Betty Crocker, and Duncan Hines introduced cake mixes after WWII, in the late 1940s and early 1950s. The popularity of cake mixes increased, especially in the 1960s and '70s, and look at what was happening in the our culture. More women were working outside the home and time was of the essence. Plus the quality of cake mixes improved. New flavors came on the scene and food magazines (with their glossy food ads) shared new recipes.

Fast-forward to current times. Yes, we do use cake mixes but we also like to replicate old-fashioned, no-packaged-mix cooking in our kitchens. These are recipes we turn to time and time again.

Cake mixes or scratch baking? Which do you prefer? The choice is yours and, either way, baking a cake is the first step toward making a delicious poke cake.

Everyday Yellow Cake

It's a one-bowl wonder! It is so simple. You mix it all in one bowl, but you get a great tasting, moist, vanilla-flavored yellow cake!

Nonstick cooking spray

2¼ cups all-purpose flour

1⅓ cups sugar

1 tablespoon baking powder

½ teaspoon salt

½ cup (1 stick) unsalted butter, softened

3 large eggs

1¼ cups whole milk

2½ teaspoons pure vanilla extract

To achieve the best results when making this cake, or any of the scratch cakes, it is important to measure all the ingredients accurately.

Preheat the oven to 350°F. Spray a 9 x 13-inch baking dish with nonstick cooking spray.

In a large bowl, whisk together the flour, sugar, baking powder, and salt. Using a handheld mixer, beat the butter into the dry ingredients on medium speed until coarse, even crumbs form. Beat in the eggs, one at a time, beating well after each addition. Add the milk and vanilla and beat for 1 minute. Pour the batter into the prepared baking dish.

Bake for 30 to 35 minutes, or until a wooden pick inserted into the center of the cake comes out clean. Place the cake on a wire rack to cool. Proceed with the poke cake recipe directions.

VARIATION

Gluten-Free Yellow Cake: Prepare the Everyday Yellow Cake as directed, substituting 2 cups gluten-free multipurpose flour blend for the all-purpose flour. Add 1 teaspoon xanthan gum along with the dry ingredients. Proceed as the recipe directs. (Testing note: Gluten-free multipurpose flour blends vary by brands. We used King Arthur brand gluten-free multipurpose flour blend for testing.)

Buttermilk White Cake

No need to worry if you don't have a cake mix on hand. This white cake comes together in just minutes.

Nonstick cooking spray
2¼ cups all-purpose flour
2 teaspoons baking soda
1½ teaspoons baking powder
½ teaspoon salt
1⅓ cups sugar
½ cup (1 stick) unsalted butter, softened
4 large egg whites
2 teaspoons pure vanilla extract
1½ cups buttermilk

TIP

No buttermilk on hand? See tip, page 8.

Preheat the oven to 350°F. Spray a 9 x 13-inch baking dish with nonstick cooking spray.

In a medium bowl, whisk together the flour, baking soda, baking powder, and salt; set aside.

In a large bowl using a handheld mixer, beat together the sugar and butter on medium-high speed until the mixture is light and creamy. Beat in the egg whites, one a time, beating well after each addition. Beat in the vanilla. Beat for 30 seconds.

Add the flour mixture, alternating with the buttermilk, making three additions of the flour and two of the buttermilk. Beat just until blended. Pour the batter into the prepared baking dish.

Bake for 33 to 38 minutes, or until a wooden pick inserted into the center comes out clean. Place the cake on a wire rack to cool. Proceed with the poke cake recipe directions.

Quick-and-Easy Chocolate Cake

Making this Quick-and-Easy Chocolate Cake is almost as effortless as opening a box of mix, but the flavor is unsurpassed. Talk about no stress! You may determine that you prefer this over a boxed cake mix every time!

Nonstick cooking spray

1 cup boiling water

2/3 cup unsweetened cocoa powder

2 cups all-purpose flour

2 cups sugar

2 teaspoons baking powder

1½ teaspoons baking soda

¼ teaspoon salt

2 large eggs

1 cup whole milk

2/3 cup canola or vegetable oil

2 teaspoons pure vanilla extract

Preheat the oven to 350°F. Spray a 9 x 13-inch baking dish with nonstick cooking spray.

In a small bowl, whisk together the boiling water and cocoa powder until smooth; set aside.

In a large bowl, whisk together the flour, sugar, baking powder, baking soda, and salt. Using a handheld mixer on low speed, beat in the eggs, milk, oil, vanilla, and the cocoa mixture. Scrape sides of the bowl well and beat for 2 minutes on medium speed. Pour the batter into the prepared baking dish.

Bake for 25 to 30 minutes, or until a wooden pick inserted into the center of the cake comes out clean. Place the cake on a wire rack to cool. Proceed with the poke cake recipe directions.

All-Time Favorite Poke Cakes

Caramel Carrot Poke Cake

This Caramel Carrot Poke Cake transforms a basic spice cake mix into a scrumptious dessert, one that is moist and studded with carrots and nuts, then topped with caramel. Shredding the carrots is as easy as using a box grater or food processor, or picking up shredded carrots in the produce section of the grocery.

Nonstick cooking spray

1 cup shredded carrots

1 (15.25- to 18-ounce) box
spice cake mix

1 (3.4-ounce) box vanilla
instant pudding mix

4 large eggs

1 cup water

⅓ cup canola or vegetable
oil

½ cup chopped walnuts,
toasted

1 cup caramel ice cream
topping

1 (8-ounce) tub frozen
whipped topping, thawed

TIP

Bags of shredded carrots are
readily available in the produce
section of grocery stores, or
you can purchase what you
need from the salad bar at the
store. To make 1 cup shredded
carrots, begin with 2 medium
carrots and shred using a box
grater or the shredding attachment on a food processor.

Preheat the oven to 350°F. Spray a 9 x 13-inch baking dish with nonstick cooking spray.

Place the shredded carrots in a medium bowl. Sprinkle the carrots with 2 tablespoons of the dry cake mix. Toss to coat the carrots evenly. Set aside.

In a large bowl, using a handheld mixer on low speed, beat together the remaining cake mix, pudding mix, eggs, water, and oil. Scrape down the sides of the bowl well and beat for 2 minutes on medium speed. Stir in the carrot mixture and walnuts.

Pour the batter into the prepared baking dish. Bake for 35 to 38 minutes, or until a wooden pick inserted into the center of the cake comes out clean. Place the cake on a wire rack and let cool completely.

Poke holes evenly over the baked cake using a drinking straw.

Drizzle ¾ cup of the caramel topping over the cake, filling all the holes.

Frost the cake with the whipped topping. Garnish the cake with the remaining caramel, drizzling and swirling it in a decorative design. Cover and refrigerate the cake for at least 1 hour or up to overnight before serving.

Hummingbird Poke Cake

Is it really made from hummingbirds? No, but Kathy's dad loved Hummingbird Cake and would always ask with a grin where one would get the hummingbirds needed for this cake. It was his favorite, and he loved laughing about the name of the cake. He would have begged for this updated version, too, for it still features the bananas, pineapple, and pecans of the original version, but the flavor soars over the top when you pour a creamy topping over the baked cake.

Nonstick cooking spray

1 (15.25- to 18-ounce) box yellow cake mix

3 large eggs

½ cup water

⅓ cup canola or vegetable oil

1 (8-ounce) can crushed pineapple in juice, not drained

2 large bananas, chopped

½ cup chopped pecans, toasted, plus more for garnish

1 (3.4-ounce) box vanilla instant pudding mix

2 cups whole milk

Cream Cheese Frosting (page 143)

Preheat the oven to 350°F. Spray a 9 x 13-inch baking dish with nonstick cooking spray.

In a large bowl using a handheld mixer on low speed, beat together the cake mix, eggs, water, oil, and crushed pineapple with the juice. Scrape down the sides of the bowl well and beat for 2 minutes on medium speed. Stir in the bananas and pecans. Pour the batter into the prepared baking dish.

Bake for 30 to 35 minutes, or until a wooden pick inserted into the center of the cake comes out clean.

Place the cake on a wire rack to cool for 10 minutes.

Poke holes evenly over the baked cake using the handle of a wooden spoon.

In a medium bowl, whisk together the pudding mix and the milk until the pudding is blended. Spoon the pudding over the cake. Use the tip of a table knife to spread the pudding evenly, filling the holes. Cover and refrigerate the cake for 1 hour.

Frost the cake with the Cream Cheese Frosting. Garnish with chopped pecans. Refrigerate until ready to serve.

Cranberry Christmas Poke Cake

Sleigh bells are jingling and the holidays are in the air. This beautiful Cranberry Christmas Poke Cake captures the flavors and colors that make the holidays festive, and gives them a whole new twist. Best of all, you can easily serve a showstopping dessert for that holiday party.

Nonstick cooking spray

1 (15.25- to 18-ounce) box white cake mix

Eggs, oil, and water as directed on the cake mix box

1 (14-ounce) can jellied cranberry sauce (not whole-berry cranberry sauce)

1 cup water

1 (3-ounce) box cranberry or raspberry gelatin

¼ cup orange juice

White Chocolate Frosting (page 149)

Preheat the oven to 350°F. Spray two 9-inch round cake pans with nonstick cooking spray. Line the bottoms of the pans with parchment paper and spray the parchment as well.

Prepare and bake the cake according to the package directions for a double-layer cake. Place the cakes on a wire rack to cool for 10 minutes.

In a small saucepan, combine the cranberry sauce and water. Heat over medium heat, stirring frequently, until the mixture boils. Use the back of a spoon or a potato masher to mash the sauce so it becomes smooth. Remove from the heat. Add the gelatin and stir until it has dissolved. Stir in the orange juice.

Poke holes evenly over the baked cakes using the handle of a wooden spoon. Slowly pour the cranberry mixture evenly over each layer, filling the holes. Use the tip of a table knife to gently push the cranberry sauce into the holes. Cover and refrigerate the cakes for 1 hour.

Place a large plate over one of the layers and invert to remove the cake from the pan. Remove the parchment paper. Use another large plate to invert the layer back so that the side with the fruit glaze remains on top. Repeat the process with second layer.

Gently spread the top of one layer with frosting. Top with the second layer, fruit-side up. Frost the top and sides of the cake. Refrigerate until ready to serve.

Cherry Cheesecake Poke Cake

Traditional cheesecake can be time-consuming to prepare. Not so with this Cherry Cheesecake Poke Cake. No need to worry about a water bath while baking or the top of the cheesecake cracking. This recipe works every time and truly is a no-brainer.

Nonstick cooking spray

2 cups graham cracker crumbs

⅓ cup sugar

½ teaspoon ground cinnamon

⅔ cup (10⅔ tablespoons) unsalted butter, melted

1 (15.25- to 18-ounce) box white cake mix

Eggs, oil, and water as directed on the cake mix box

1 (8-ounce) package cream cheese, softened

1 (14-ounce) can sweetened condensed milk

1 (3.4-ounce) box cheesecake instant pudding mix

¾ cup whole milk

1 (30-ounce) can cherry pie filling

Preheat the oven to 350°F. Spray a 9 x 13-inch baking dish with nonstick cooking spray.

In a medium bowl, stir together graham cracker crumbs, sugar, and cinnamon. Pour melted butter over the mixture and stir to combine. Pour into the prepared baking dish and press evenly over the bottom of the pan.

Prepare the cake batter according to the package directions. Pour the batter over the crumb crust in the baking dish. Bake according to the package directions for a 9 x 13-inch cake. Place the cake on a wire rack and let cool completely.

Poke holes evenly over the baked cake using the handle of a wooden spoon.

In a large bowl, using a handheld mixer on medium-high speed, beat the cream cheese, sweetened condensed milk, pudding mix, and milk until smooth.

Pour the cream cheese filling evenly over the cake and use the tip of a butter knife to spread the filling to fill all the holes. Cover and refrigerate for 1 hour.

Spoon the cherry pie filling evenly over the cake. Serve immediately or refrigerate until ready to serve.

TIP

Substitute vanilla instant pudding for cheesecake instant pudding.

Red Velvet Poke Cake

We doubt there has ever been a Junior League soiree in the South that didn't include a version of Red Velvet Cake. Red Velvet Cake has strong ties to the South, and if it didn't show up in the local Junior League cookbook, you can rest assured it was a star player at the church potluck. It's high time this iconic recipe has a makeover that ensures ease and entertainment. No fuss, no frills, just great-tasting goodness.

Nonstick cooking spray
1 (15.25- to 18-ounce) box red velvet cake mix
Eggs, oil, and water as directed on the cake mix box
1 (8-ounce) package cream cheese, softened
¾ cup sweetened condensed milk
1 cup confectioners' sugar
3 tablespoons whole milk
1 teaspoon pure vanilla extract
Almond Cream Cheese Frosting (page 143)
Coarse red decorating sugar, for garnish (optional)

TIP

For a spectacular presentation, top the cake with curls of white chocolate.

Preheat the oven to 350°F. Spray a 9 x 13-inch baking dish with nonstick cooking spray.

Prepare and bake the cake according to the package directions for a 9 x 13-inch cake. Place the cake on a wire rack to cool for 10 minutes.

In a large bowl using a handheld mixer on medium-high speed, beat the cream cheese, sweetened condensed milk, confectioners' sugar, whole milk, and vanilla until smooth.

Poke holes evenly over the baked cake using a drinking straw. Pour the cream cheese filling evenly over the cake and use the tip of a butter knife to spread to fill all the holes. Cover and refrigerate the cake for 1 hour.

Frost the cake with the Almond Cream Cheese Frosting. If desired, sprinkle with decorating sugar. Refrigerate until ready to serve.

Confetti Poke 'n' Tote Cakes

It's party time! Pack these portable Confetti Poke 'n' Tote Cakes in a cooler and take them to your next event. They are easy to make, they look oh so cute, and they are fun to eat. What more could you want? How about make-ahead convenience? You can make these the day before the party and avoid the last-minute rush.

Nonstick cooking spray

1½ cups all-purpose flour

2 teaspoons rainbow sprinkles, plus more for garnish

1½ teaspoons baking powder

¼ teaspoon salt

¾ cup sugar

6 tablespoons (¾ stick) unsalted butter, softened

2 large eggs

2 teaspoons pure vanilla extract

1 cup whole milk

1 cup water

1 (3-ounce) box strawberry gelatin

½ cup cold water

1 (8-ounce) tub frozen whipped topping, thawed, or Vanilla Buttercream Frosting (page 144)

Preheat the oven to 350°F. Spray 12 (8-ounce) canning jars with nonstick cooking spray. Set the canning jar lids and rings aside.

Measure out 1 tablespoon of the flour into a small bowl. Mix in 2 teaspoons sprinkles; set aside.

In a small bowl, whisk together the remaining flour, the baking powder, and the salt; set aside.

In a large bowl using a handheld mixer on medium-high speed, beat together the sugar and the butter until the mixture is light and creamy. Beat in the eggs, one a time, beating well after each addition.

In a measuring cup, mix the vanilla into the milk. Add the flour mixture to the butter mixture, alternating with the milk, making three additions of the flour and two of the milk. Add the flour-sprinkles mixture along with the last addition of flour. Beat just until blended.

Spoon about ¼ cup of the batter into each of the prepared jars. Do not cover.

Arrange the jars in a shallow baking pan, leaving about 1 inch between the jars. Bake for 24 to 28 minutes, or until a wooden pick inserted into the center of the cakes comes out clean. (Do not overbake.) Place the baking pan with the jars in it on a wire rack and let the cakes cool completely.

Poke holes evenly over the baked cakes in the jars using the tines of a fork.

Place the 1 cup water in a 4-cup microwave-safe glass bowl. Microwave on High (100%) power for 2 to 3 minutes, or until the water comes to a boil. Stir the gelatin into the water until it is dissolved. Stir in the ½ cup cold water. Spoon about 2 tablespoons of the gelatin over the cake in each jar. Seal each jar with its lid and ring and refrigerate the cakes for 1 hour.

Uncover the jars and dollop or pipe whipped topping or frosting on top of each cake. Garnish with sprinkles. Seal each jar again and refrigerate until ready to serve.

VARIATIONS

Poke Cupcakes: Line muffin pans with paper liners. Prepare the batter as directed and spoon it into the prepared pan, filling each cup about halfway full. Bake for 15 to 18 minutes, or until a wooden pick inserted into the center of the cakes comes out clean. Proceed as the recipe directs, poking the cupcakes with a fork, drizzling with gelatin, and dolloping with whipped topping or frosting.

Individual Poke Cakes: Instead of canning jars, prepare the individual poke cakes in 8-ounce oven-proof ramekins. Bake for 15 to 18 minutes, or until a wooden pick inserted into the center of the cakes comes out clean. Proceed as the recipe directs, poking with a fork, drizzling with gelatin, and dolloping with whipped topping or frosting.

❋ Use caution when testing the cake for doneness or removing the pan of jars from the oven, as the jars will be hot.

❋ Substitute any flavor of gelatin you prefer, or match the color of a party with the color of the gelatin.

❋ Pack the Poke 'n' Tote Cakes in a cooler with ice packs to transport them to a park or other outside event. Use ribbon or string to tie a plastic spoon to each jar.

Candy Bar Poke Cake

Roxanne cherishes get-togethers with her extended family. The more nieces and nephews, the happier she is. The memory of a celebration by the lake and the squeals of delight that the littlest one made when she carried a Candy Bar Poke Cake to the picnic table will forever bring a smile to her face. If you are going to a party or dinner where there will be toddlers, tweens, and teenagers, this recipe is your ticket to great fun and laughter.

Nonstick cooking spray

1 (15.25- to 18-ounce) box devil's food cake mix

Eggs, oil, and water as directed on the cake mix box

1 (14-ounce) can sweetened condensed milk

1 (12.25-ounce) jar caramel ice cream topping

1 (8-ounce) tub frozen whipped topping, thawed

8 (1.5- to 1.9-ounce) candy bars, coarsely chopped (see Tip)

Preheat the oven to 350°F. Spray a 9 x 13-inch baking dish with nonstick cooking spray.

Prepare and bake the cake according to the package directions for a 9 x 13-inch cake. Place the cake on a wire rack to cool for 10 minutes.

Poke holes evenly over the baked cake using the tines of a fork.

In a small bowl, stir together the sweetened condensed milk and the caramel ice cream topping. Pour the mixture evenly over the cake. Cover and refrigerate the cake for 1 hour.

Frost the cake with the whipped topping and sprinkle the chopped candy evenly over the top. Refrigerate until ready to serve.

TIPS

❋ You can use any favorite chocolate cake mix for this crowd-pleasing cake.

❋ Use a variety of candy bars including peanut butter cups, KitKats, M&M's, and crunchy Butterfingers.

Cannoli Poke Cake

A cannoli is a favorite dessert at the Italian restaurants all over town, and is there anyone who doesn't love ordering them when eating out? The crisp shells and creamy filling can't be beat, but frying those shells at home may be a little daunting. Now you can capture that flavor with this easy Cannoli Poke Cake. The crunchy-crisp cookies on the top will remind you of crisp cannoli shells.

Nonstick cooking spray

1 (15.25- to 18-ounce) box white cake mix

1 (3.4-ounce) box vanilla instant pudding mix

4 large eggs

1 cup water

⅓ cup canola or vegetable oil

1 (14-ounce) can sweetened condensed milk

CANNOLI POKE CAKE FROSTING:

1 cup heavy cream

1 (8-ounce) package cream cheese, softened

1 cup confectioners' sugar

2 tablespoons whole milk

½ teaspoon ground cinnamon

½ teaspoon pure vanilla extract

Mini semisweet chocolate chips, for garnish

12 to 15 French vanilla or chocolate hazelnut-filled rolled cookies, sliced into ¼-inch pieces, for garnish

Preheat the oven to 350°F. Spray a 9 x 13-inch baking dish with nonstick cooking spray.

In a large bowl using a handheld mixer on low speed, beat together the cake mix, pudding mix, eggs, water, and oil. Scrape down sides of the bowl well and beat for 2 minutes on medium speed. Pour the batter into the prepared baking dish.

Bake for 25 to 30 minutes, or until a wooden pick inserted into the center of the cake comes out clean.

Put the cake on a wire rack to cool for 10 minutes.

Poke holes evenly over the baked cake using a drinking straw. Pour the sweetened condensed milk slowly and evenly over the cake. Cover and refrigerate the cake for 1 hour.

MAKE THE CANNOLI POKE CAKE FROSTING: In a medium bowl using a handheld mixer on low speed, beat the cream until frothy. Increase speed to medium-high and beat until stiff peaks form. Set the whipped cream aside.

In a separate medium bowl using a handheld mixer on medium-high speed, beat together the cream cheese and confectioners' sugar until light and fluffy. Beat in the milk, cinnamon, and vanilla until smooth. Using a spatula, gently fold in the whipped cream.

Frost the cake with the frosting. Garnish with the mini chocolate chips. Cover and refrigerate the cake for at least 1 hour or up to overnight.

Just before serving, sprinkle the cake with the cookies.

❄ This frosting is softer than some frostings. The texture is more reminiscent of the soft, creamy filling used in cannoli.

❄ Sprinkle the cake with the crisp cookie pieces just before serving, or the cookies will become soggy. If you are not planning to serve all the cake at once, cut the cake into pieces and sprinkle each piece of cake with the cookies as you serve it.

❄ What are those rolled cookies? Look for these pastry-like, rolled, and filled wafer cookies with the packaged cookies. We prefer to use Pepperidge Farm Pirouette Cookies with either the French vanilla or chocolate-hazelnut filling.

❄ Cannoli are often traditionally filled with a ricotta filling. If you wish to make this cake more classic in flavor, drain 1 (16-ounce) tub whole-milk ricotta cheese and substitute it for the cream cheese in the frosting, then proceed as the recipe directs.

Pistachio Poke Cake

We can tell your age if you remember the version of this cake that became famous and was served frequently during the Watergate scandal. Both the cake and a salad by the same name adorned the table of every potluck during the mid-seventies to early eighties. If you are too young to remember all the hoopla, suffice it to say that the cake was supposedly named Watergate due to the amount of nuts it contained and the fluffy texture. No matter the origin, this recipe needs to be remembered for years to come.

Nonstick cooking spray
1 (15.25- to 18-ounce) box
 white cake mix
3 large eggs
2 (3.4-ounce) boxes pistachio
 instant pudding mix
1 cup canola or vegetable oil
1 cup lemon-lime-flavored
 soda
1 cup chopped pecans,
 toasted
1 cup sweetened shredded
 or flaked coconut
2 cups whole milk
1 (8-ounce) tub frozen
 whipped topping, thawed

Preheat the oven to 350°F. Spray a 9 x 13-inch baking dish with nonstick cooking spray.

In a large bowl using a handheld mixer on low speed, beat together the cake mix, eggs, 1 box pudding mix, the oil, and the lemon-lime soda. Scrape down the sides of the bowl well and beat for 2 minutes on medium speed. Stir in ½ cup of the pecans and ½ cup of the coconut. Pour the batter into prepared baking dish. Bake for 35 to 40 minutes, or until a wooden pick inserted into the center of the cake comes out clean.

Place the cake on a wire rack and let cool completely.

Poke holes evenly over the baked cake using the handle of a wooden spoon.

In a medium bowl, whisk together the remaining box of pudding mix and the milk. Pour evenly over the cake, filling the holes. Cover and refrigerate for 1 hour.

Place the remaining ½ cup coconut in a dry skillet over medium heat. Stir continuously until the coconut is toasted. Remove from the heat and allow to cool completely.

Frost the cake with the whipped topping. Sprinkle with the remaining ½ cup pecans and the toasted coconut. Refrigerate until ready to serve.

Rainbow Poke Cake

There is something about this Rainbow Poke Cake that screams PARTY! You don't need an excuse to celebrate; get in the kitchen and have fun. Your friends and family will enjoy the fruits of your labor and you don't have to tell them how easy this is to create.

Nonstick cooking spray

1 (15.25- to 18-ounce) box white or vanilla cake mix

Eggs, oil, and water as directed on the cake mix box

3 cups water

1 (3-ounce) box lime gelatin

1 (3-ounce) box berry blue gelatin

1 (3-ounce) box strawberry gelatin

Easy Decorator's Frosting (page 148), or 1 (8-ounce) tub frozen whipped topping, thawed

Sprinkles or jimmies

You can vary the colors of the rainbow by using different flavors of gelatin. Select the colors that you prefer.

Preheat the oven to 350°F. Spray a 9 x 13-inch baking dish with nonstick cooking spray.

Prepare and bake the cake according to the package directions for a 9 x 13-inch pan. Place the cake on a wire rack and let cool for 20 minutes.

Poke holes evenly over the baked cake using the tines of a fork.

Place 1 cup of the water in a 4-cup microwave-safe glass bowl. Microwave on High (100%) power for 2 to 3 minutes, or until the water comes to a boil. Stir the lime gelatin into the water until it has dissolved. Using a separate bowl for each, repeat with the berry blue and strawberry gelatin, using 1 cup of the remaining water for each.

Pour each gelatin mixture down the cake to form three long rows. Cover and refrigerate the cake for 1 hour.

Frost the cake with Easy Decorator's Frosting or whipped topping. Sprinkle the sprinkles or jimmies over the top of the cake. Refrigerate until ready to serve.

Pralines and Cream Poke Cake

You don't need to travel to the French Quarter in New Orleans to experience the sweet pecan crunch of pralines and that indescribable caramel flavor. Bake a Pralines and Cream Poke Cake in a snap, then enjoy a slice while you linger sipping chicory coffee. Laissez les bon temps roulez, as they say in the Crescent City— "Let the good times roll!"

Nonstick cooking spray
1 (15.25- to 18-ounce) box butter pecan cake mix
Eggs, oil, and water as directed on the cake mix box
½ cup butterscotch ice cream topping
Caramel Frosting (page 145)
¾ cup coarsely chopped pecans, toasted

Preheat the oven to 350°F. Spray a 9 x 13-inch baking dish with nonstick cooking spray.

Prepare and bake the cake according to the package directions for a 9 x 13-inch cake. Place the cake on a wire rack to cool for 10 minutes.

Poke holes evenly over the baked cake using the tines of a fork. Pour the butterscotch topping evenly over the cake.

Frost the cake with the Caramel Frosting. Immediately sprinkle with the pecans and gently press the pecans into the frosting using the back of a large spoon.

TIPS

✳ Substitute caramel-flavored topping for butterscotch.

✳ Substitute a yellow, vanilla, or white cake mix for the butter pecan cake mix.

Applesauce Poke Cake with Maple-Cinnamon Sauce

You can almost taste the comfort in each bite of this Applesauce Poke Cake. Maple syrup, applesauce, spices, and pecans make a perfect combo. Sure, applesauce cakes are excellent desserts to serve in the fall, but this old-fashioned flavor just might become your year-round favorite cake.

Nonstick cooking spray

1 (15.25- to 18-ounce) box yellow cake mix

1½ cups unsweetened applesauce

3 large eggs

½ cup (1 stick) plus 2 tablespoons unsalted butter, melted

½ cup chopped pecans, toasted, plus more, if desired, for garnish

½ cup maple syrup or maple-flavored pancake syrup

1 teaspoon ground cinnamon

1½ cups heavy cream

3 tablespoons confectioners' sugar

Preheat the oven to 350°F. Spray a 9 x 13-inch baking dish with nonstick cooking spray.

In a large bowl using a handheld mixer on low speed, beat together the cake mix, applesauce, eggs, and ½ cup of the melted butter. Scrape down the sides of the bowl well and beat for 2 minutes on medium speed. Stir in the pecans. Pour the batter into the prepared baking dish.

Bake for 30 to 35 minutes, or until a wooden pick inserted into the center of the cake comes out clean. Place the cake on a wire rack to cool for 10 minutes.

Poke holes evenly over the baked cake using the tines of a fork.

Blend together the maple syrup, the remaining 2 tablespoons melted butter, and the cinnamon. Slowly drizzle the maple syrup mixture over the cake. Let the cake cool completely.

In a medium bowl using a handheld mixer, beat the cream on low speed until frothy. Increase the speed to medium-high. Gradually add the confectioners' sugar, beating continuously until the cream holds stiff peaks.

Frost the cake with the whipped cream. Garnish with chopped pecans, if desired. Refrigerate until ready to serve.

 TIPS

⁕ Substitute 1 (8-ounce) tub frozen whipped topping, thawed, for the heavy cream and confectioners' sugar, if desired.

⁕ Maple syrup or pancake syrup? Either syrup works well. Real maple syrup is a natural, great-tasting syrup. Pancake syrup is flavored to taste like maple. Either syrup works well in this recipe.

Patriotic Poke Cake

There are so many holidays and special occasions to demonstrate your patriotic pride. Bake Patriotic Poke Cake to celebrate the "rockets' red glare." Celebrate someone you care about who has served our country in the military and bake a thank-you that is sure to mean more than words. Ignite pride in our country around the dessert table and celebrate the many blessings of freedom.

Nonstick cooking spray

1 (15.25- to 18-ounce) box white cake mix

Eggs, oil, and water as directed on the cake mix box

2 cups water

1 (3-ounce) box strawberry gelatin

1 (3-ounce) box berry blue gelatin

Easy Decorator's Frosting (page 148)

TIPS

❊ Be sure to remove the parchment paper from the baked cakes before frosting.

Decorate the top of the cake with red and blue sprinkles, if desired.

Preheat the oven to 350°F. Spray two 9-inch round cake pans with nonstick cooking spray. Line the bottoms of the pans with parchment paper cut to fit and spray the parchment as well.

Prepare and bake the cake according to the package directions for a double-layer cake. Place the cakes on a wire rack to cool for 10 minutes.

Place 1 cup of the water in a 4-cup microwave-safe glass bowl. Microwave on High (100%) power for 2 to 3 minutes, or until the water comes to a boil. Stir the strawberry gelatin into the water until it has dissolved. Using a separate bowl, repeat with the berry blue gelatin.

Poke holes evenly over both of the baked cakes using the tines of a fork. Pour the strawberry gelatin over one cake layer and the berry blue gelatin over the other cake layer. Cover and refrigerate the cakes for 1 hour.

Remove the layer cakes from the refrigerator. Place a large plate over one of the layers and invert to remove the cake from the pan. Remove the parchment paper. Use another large plate to invert the layer back so that the side with the gelatin remains on top. Repeat the process with the second layer. Spread the top of one layer with a thin layer of Easy Decorator's Frosting. Top with the second layer. Frost the top and sides with the remaining Easy Decorator's Frosting. Refrigerate until ready to serve.

White Chocolate-Raspberry Poke Cake

White chocolate is not truly chocolate, but that's okay since it still tastes so good and is very pretty. White Chocolate-Raspberry Poke Cake is a prime example, as the beautiful creamy white cake and frosting, contrasting with the ruby red raspberry poke, makes this cake both gorgeous and tasty. This delicious cake will be the star no matter when you serve it!

Nonstick cooking spray

2 ounces white chocolate, chopped

1 (15.25- to 18-ounce) box white cake mix

⅓ cup canola or vegetable oil

1 cup sour cream

4 large eggs

1 cup water

½ cup seedless raspberry jam

1 (3-ounce) box raspberry gelatin

⅔ cup cold water

White Chocolate Frosting (page 149)

Preheat the oven to 350°F. Spray a 9 x 13-inch baking dish with nonstick cooking spray.

Melt the white chocolate according to the package directions. Let cool until just warm.

In a large bowl using a handheld mixer on low speed, beat together the cake mix, oil, sour cream, eggs, and melted white chocolate. Scrape down the sides of the bowl well and beat for 2 minutes on medium speed.

Pour the batter into the prepared baking dish. Bake for 30 to 35 minutes, or until a wooden pick inserted into the center of the cake comes out clean. Place the cake on a wire rack and let cool completely.

Poke holes evenly over the baked cake using the tines of a fork.

Place the 1 cup water in a 4-cup microwave-safe glass bowl. Microwave on High (100%) power for 2 to 3 minutes or until the water comes to a boil. Stir the jam into the boiling water and continue stirring until the jam has melted. Microwave the mixture on high for 20 seconds, or until the water begins to boil again. Stir the gelatin into the water until it has dissolved. Stir in the 2/3 cup cold water.

Slowly pour the raspberry gelatin mixture evenly over the cake, filling the holes. If necessary, use the tip of a butter knife to gently spread any bits of raspberry jam evenly over the top of the cake. Cover and refrigerate the cake for 1 hour.

Frost the cake with the White Chocolate Frosting. Refrigerate until ready to serve.

Coconut Cream Poke Cake

Who wouldn't love a dreamy cake that looks as if it is floating on pillows in the clouds? The sweetness of coconut and the creamy filling come together to form the perfect match. (We keep cream of coconut on hand and prefer to purchase the pourable 22-ounce variety; no waste and we can measure out what we need when we need it.) No worries about a flaky crust with this recipe. The proof is in the pudding!

Nonstick cooking spray
1 (15.25- to 18-ounce) box
  white cake mix
1 cup sour cream
½ cup canola or vegetable
  oil
3 large eggs
1 teaspoon pure vanilla
  extract
¾ cup cream of coconut
1 (5.1-ounce) box vanilla
  instant pudding mix
3 cups whole milk
1 (8-ounce) tub frozen
  whipped topping, thawed
1 cup sweetened shredded
  or flaked coconut

Preheat the oven to 350°F. Spray a 9 x 13-inch baking dish with nonstick cooking spray.

In a large bowl using a handheld mixer on low speed, beat together the cake mix, sour cream, oil, eggs, and vanilla. Scrape down the sides of the bowl well and beat for 2 minutes on medium speed. Pour the batter into the prepared baking dish.

Bake for 28 to 30 minutes, or until a wooden pick inserted into the center of the cake comes out clean. Place the cake on a wire rack. Poke holes evenly over the baked cake using a drinking straw. While the cake is still warm, drizzle the cream of coconut evenly over the cake, filling the poked holes. Let the cake cool completely.

In a medium bowl, whisk together the pudding mix and the milk until the pudding is blended. Spread the pudding evenly over the cake. Carefully spread the whipped topping over the pudding layer. Sprinkle the cake evenly with the coconut. Cover and refrigerate for at least 1 hour or up to overnight before serving.

TIPS

✳ This cake is best made the day ahead. It will keep in refrigerator for up to 1 week.

✳ For a colorful garnish, drain 12 maraschino cherries and pat dry with a paper towel. Place the cherries on the cake, spacing them evenly, making four rows with three cherries in each row. When serving, cut the cake into twelve squares with a cherry in the middle of each slice.

✳ If you prefer the crunchiness of toasted coconut, feel free to toast the coconut and then sprinkle it on top. To toast coconut, preheat the oven to 350°F. Spread the coconut evenly over a rimmed baking sheet. Bake, stirring occasionally, for 7 to 8 minutes, or until light golden brown. Let cool completely before sprinkling on the cake.

Chai Poke Cake

We never really understood what all the fuss about chai was—until we tasted Chai Poke Cake. When you think about it, it makes sense. Chai is essentially a spiced milk from India that is usually made up of tea, milk, spices, and a sweetener. It is known to provide a sense of well-being. Enjoy a slice of this spice-infused cake and you, too, can enjoy calm and well-being in your daily life.

2 cups whole milk

4 chai tea bags

Nonstick cooking spray

1 (15.25- to 18-ounce) box spice cake mix

Eggs, oil, and water as directed on the cake mix box

1 (3.4-ounce) box vanilla instant pudding mix

1 (8-ounce) tub frozen whipped topping, thawed

TIP

If desired, sprinkle the finished cake lightly with ground cinnamon.

In a small saucepan, heat the milk over medium heat until it begins to simmer. Immediately remove from the heat and pour into a heatproof 4-cup measure or 4-cup heatproof glass bowl. Add the tea bags and steep for 10 minutes. Remove and discard the tea bags. Let the milk mixture cool to room temperature while you prepare and bake the cake.

Preheat the oven to 350°F. Spray a 9 x13-inch baking dish with nonstick cooking spray.

Prepare and bake the cake according to the package directions for a 9 x 13-inch cake. Place the cake on a wire rack to cool for 10 minutes.

Poke holes evenly over the baked cake using the handle of a wooden spoon.

In a medium bowl, whisk together the pudding mix and the chai milk until the pudding is blended. Pour the pudding evenly over the top of the cake, spreading it evenly and filling in the poked holes. Cover and refrigerate the cake for 1 hour.

Frost the cake with the whipped topping. Cover and refrigerate the cake for at least 1 hour or up to overnight before serving.

Tres Leches Poke Cake

Tres leches cake, or "three milk" cake, is especially popular in Central and South America and, yes, it really uses three different milk products—cream, evaporated milk, and sweetened condensed milk. We love one possible story regarding the history of the cake. This popular cake may have originated over one hundred years ago and may have first appeared on the label for one of the canned milks. Imagine our delight to learn that, as we've spent much of our professional careers developing recipes for companies to print on food labels and packages. That is a successful recipe!

Nonstick cooking spray

1 (15.25- to 18-ounce) white cake mix

Eggs and oil as directed on the cake mix box

Buttermilk, in place of the water called for on the cake mix box

½ cup heavy cream

1 (14-ounce) can sweetened condensed milk

1 (5-ounce) can evaporated milk

2 teaspoons pure vanilla extract

TRES LECHES VANILLA CREAM TOPPING:

1½ cups heavy cream

¼ cup confectioners' sugar

1 teaspoon pure vanilla extract

Preheat the oven to 350°F. Spray a 9 x 13-inch baking dish with nonstick cooking spray.

Prepare the cake according to the package directions, substituting buttermilk for the water called for on the box. Bake according to the package directions for a 9 x 13-inch cake.

Place the cake on a wire rack and let cool completely.

Poke holes evenly over the baked cake using the tines of a fork.

In a medium bowl, stir together the cream, sweetened condensed milk, evaporated milk, and vanilla. Slowly and evenly pour the milk mixture over the cake. Cover and refrigerate the cake for 1 hour.

MAKE THE TRES LECHES VANILLA CREAM TOPPING: In a medium bowl using a handheld mixer, beat the cream on low speed until frothy. Increase the speed to medium-high. Gradually beat in the confectioners' sugar, beating continuously until the cream holds stiff peaks. Beat in the vanilla.

Frost the cake with the whipped cream. Cover and refrigerate for at least 1 hour or up to overnight before serving.

 TIP Substitute 1 (8-ounce) tub frozen whipped topping, thawed, for the Tres Leches Vanilla Cream Topping.

Blue Moon Poke Cake

What can we say? This is silly, right? But the child in all of us loves to play with the colors of our food. Remember the popularity of Green Eggs and Ham? *Do you know any preschooler who won't think you are "over the moon" for baking this Blue Moon Poke Cake to enjoy? And if you want to go all-out, the sprinkles are a fun garnish.*

Nonstick cooking spray

1 (15.25- to 18-ounce) box white cake mix

Eggs, oil, and water as directed on the cake mix box

1 (0.22-ounce) unsweetened blue raspberry lemonade drink mix

1 cup sugar

1 cup water

Easy Decorator's Frosting (page 148)

Blue food coloring

Preheat the oven to 350°F. Spray a 9 x 13-inch baking dish with nonstick cooking spray.

Prepare and bake the cake according to the package directions for a 9 x 13-inch cake. Place the cake on a wire rack to cool for 5 to 10 minutes.

While cake is baking, in a small saucepan, stir together the drink mix, sugar, and water. Heat the mixture over medium-high heat until it just begins to boil; remove from the heat and let cool slightly.

Poke holes evenly over the baked cake using the tines of a fork. Pour the blue mixture evenly over the cake. Let the cake cool completely.

Prepare the Easy Decorator's Frosting and stir in a few drops of blue food coloring to achieve a bright blue color. Frost the cake with the frosting. Refrigerate until ready to serve.

Blue Moon Poke Cake (continued)

TIPS

❋ Scatter cake sprinkles evenly over the cake top for a festive appearance.

❋ Substitute your favorite color of unsweetened drink mix for the pourable poke portion, then color the Easy Decorator's Frosting with food coloring to match.

❋ If you are dealing with a lack of time, omit the Easy Decorator Frosting and frost the cake with 1 (8-ounce) tub frozen whipped topping, thawed. You can add blue food coloring to the whipped topping, if desired. Refrigerate the cake until ready to serve.

Shirley Temple Poke Cake

The Shirley Temple nonalcoholic cocktail was allegedly served to the child star at the age of ten when she was celebrating her birthday at the Beverly Hills restaurant Chasen's. It became one of the most popular nonalcoholic drinks of all time. There is some question as to whether this is the true origin of the famous drink, but the story really doesn't matter once you take a bite of this Shirley Temple Poke Cake, developed to resemble the taste of the Shirley Temple drink.

Nonstick cooking spray
1 (15.25- to 18-ounce) box white cake mix
Eggs and oil as directed on the cake mix box
¾ cup lemon-lime-flavored soda, plus additional water to equal the amount of liquid specified on the box
½ cup plus 3 tablespoons grenadine syrup
1 (8-ounce) tub frozen whipped topping, thawed
Maraschino cherries, drained, for garnish (optional)

Preheat the oven to 350°F. Spray a 9 x 13-inch baking dish with nonstick cooking spray.

Prepare the cake according to the package directions, substituting the lemon-lime soda and water mixture for the water called for on the box. Bake according to the package directions for a 9 x 13-inch pan. Place the cake on a wire rack and let cool for 20 minutes.

Poke holes evenly over the baked cake using the tines of a fork.

Drizzle ½ cup of the grenadine into the holes. Cover and refrigerate for 1 hour.

In a medium bowl, combine the thawed whipped topping and remaining 3 tablespoons grenadine. Frost the cake with the whipped topping mixture. Refrigerate until ready to serve.

Cut into servings and garnish each serving with a maraschino cherry, if desired.

TIPS

⁕ If desired, substitute stiffly beaten sweetened whipped cream for the whipped topping. In a medium bowl, beat 1½ cups heavy cream with a handheld mixer on low speed until frothy. Increase the speed to medium-high. Gradually beat in 3 tablespoons confectioners' sugar; beat until the cream holds stiff peaks. Proceed as directed in the recipe.

⁕ Grenadine is a sweet red syrup that is often used to flavor cocktails. While it is not a liquor, you will often find it in the grocery store shelved with mixers and supplies for cocktails. A substitute for grenadine could be maraschino cherry juice.

Cappuccino Poke Cake

Cappuccino, lattes, and other coffee drinks took the country by storm a few years back when Starbucks and other shops began flavoring, frothing, and decorating the delicious hot drinks. Now, if baristas had a competition on what to serve with those coffee drinks, this delicious Cappuccino Poke Cake would surely win. Pour a cup and enjoy a piece of this poke cake.

Nonstick cooking spray

1 (15.25- to 18-ounce) box dark chocolate cake mix

3 large eggs

1 cup sour cream

½ cup whole milk

¼ cup canola or vegetable oil

2 teaspoons instant espresso powder

1 (8-ounce) tub frozen whipped topping, thawed

CREAMY ESPRESSO SAUCE:

¼ cup heavy cream

½ teaspoon instant espresso powder

1 cup vanilla chips

Preheat the oven to 350°F. Spray a 9 x 13-inch baking dish with nonstick cooking spray.

In a large bowl using a handheld mixer on low speed, beat together the cake mix, eggs, sour cream, milk, oil, and espresso powder. Scrape down the sides of the bowl well and beat for 2 minutes on medium speed. Pour the batter into the prepared baking dish.

Bake for 30 to 35 minutes, or until a wooden pick inserted into the center of the cake comes out clean.

Place the cake on a wire rack to cool for 10 minutes.

MAKE THE CREAMY ESPRESSO SAUCE: In a 2-cup microwave-safe glass bowl, stir together the heavy cream and espresso powder to combine. Stir in the vanilla chips. Microwave on Medium (50%) power in 30-second intervals, stirring after each, until melted and smooth.

Poke holes evenly over the baked cake using a drinking straw. Slowly pour the Creamy Espresso Sauce over the cake, filling all the holes. Let cool completely.

Frost the cake with the whipped topping. Cover and refrigerate for at least 1 hour or up to overnight before serving.

TIPS

❋ Substitute Vanilla Buttercream Frosting (page 144) or White Chocolate Frosting (page 149) for the frozen whipped topping, if desired.

❋ Do you like your cappuccino flavored? If so, stir 2 tablespoons flavored liquid coffee creamer into the warm and melted Creamy Espresso Sauce. Choose flavors such as hazelnut or amaretto, or use your favorite flavor.

❋ Garnish the top of the cake with chocolate-covered espresso beans, if desired.

Cinnamon Roll Poke Loaf

Nostalgia is a hot topic today. Everyone seems to enjoy remembering the good old days. Can you blame them? Times seemed simpler back then, with no cell phones, text messages, Twitter feeds to read, and so on. When you need to check out of the tech world and revisit your past, why not invite some friends over for coffee? Yes, that's right, invite friends to chat, catch up, and linger over coffee and a slice of this cinnamon-infused delight. There, now, everything becomes clearer and life is good!

Nonstick cooking spray

1 (16-ounce) box pound cake mix

⅓ cup plus 2 tablespoons cinnamon roll–flavored liquid coffee creamer

⅓ cup water

½ cup (1 stick) unsalted butter, softened

2 large eggs

¼ cup sugar

2 teaspoons ground cinnamon

½ cup coarsely chopped pecans, toasted

CINNAMON ROLL CAKE ICING:

2½ cups confectioners' sugar

3 to 4 tablespoons cinnamon roll–flavored liquid coffee creamer

Preheat the oven to 350°F. Spray a 9 x 5-inch loaf pan with nonstick cooking spray.

In a large bowl using a handheld mixer on low speed, beat together the pound cake mix, ⅓ cup of the flavored creamer, the water, butter, and eggs. Scrape down the sides of the bowl well and beat for 2 minutes on medium speed.

In a small bowl, stir together the sugar, cinnamon, and pecans. Pour half the pound cake batter into the prepared pan. Sprinkle the surface evenly with about one-third of the sugar-cinnamon mixture. Pour half the remaining batter over the sugar-cinnamon mixture. Sprinkle evenly with a third of the sugar-cinnamon mixture. Pour the remaining batter evenly over all. Sprinkle with the remaining sugar-cinnamon mixture.

Bake for 50 to 60 minutes, or until a wooden pick inserted into the center of the cake comes out clean. Place the cake on a wire rack to cool for 5 minutes.

Poke holes about 1 inch apart evenly over the baked cake using a skewer. Drizzle the remaining 2 tablespoons flavored creamer evenly over the cake, allowing the creamer to soak into the poked holes. Let the loaf cool completely.

(continued)

MAKE THE CINNAMON ROLL CAKE ICING: In a medium bowl, combine the confectioners' sugar and the flavored creamer until you reach a thick but pourable consistency. Place the icing in a zip-top bag and clip off the corner.

Remove the cake from the pan and place on a serving plate. Drizzle the icing over the top of the cooled cake to cover the surface, allowing some icing to drizzle down the sides. Let icing set up, about 5 to 10 minutes, before serving.

Boston Cream Poke Cake

Boston cream pie is a classic, but strange as it is, it is a cake and not a pie. The dessert, dating from the 1850s, was developed by a pastry chef at the Parker House Hotel in Boston. The delicious cake was topped with pastry cream and chocolate. Now we have updated that timeless dessert into an easy-to-make Boston Cream Poke Cake. You will especially love the chocolate ganache that tops the pudding in this dessert.

Nonstick cooking spray

1 (15.25- to 18-ounce) butter recipe yellow cake mix or plain yellow cake mx

Eggs, butter (or oil), and water as directed on the cake mix box

1 (5.1-ounce) box vanilla instant pudding mix

2½ cups whole milk

2 teaspoons pure vanilla extract

¾ cup heavy cream

6 tablespoons (¾ stick) unsalted butter, cut into pieces

1½ cups semisweet chocolate chips

2 tablespoons confectioners' sugar

CHOCOLATE GANACHE:

¾ cup heavy cream

6 tablespoons (¾ stick) unsalted butter

1½ cups semisweet chocolate chips

1 teaspoon pure vanilla extract

2 tablespoons confectioners' sugar

Preheat the oven to 350°F. Spray a 9 x 13-inch baking dish with nonstick cooking spray.

Prepare and bake the cake according to the package directions for a 9 x 13-inch cake. Place the cake on a wire rack and let cool completely.

Poke holes evenly over the baked cake using a drinking straw.

In a medium bowl, whisk together the pudding mix with the milk until the pudding is blended. Stir in 1 teaspoon of the vanilla. Pour the pudding over the top of the cake, spreading it evenly and filling in the poked holes. Cover and refrigerate the cake for 1 hour.

MAKE THE CHOCOLATE GANACHE: Place the heavy cream and the butter in a medium microwave-safe glass bowl. Microwave on High (100%) power for 50 to 60 seconds or until the cream begins to boil and the butter melts.

Stir the chocolate chips into the hot cream mixture until the chips are melted. Stir in the vanilla and the confectioners' sugar. Continue to stir until smooth.

Pour the chocolate ganache over the pudding layer, covering the pudding completely.

Cover and refrigerate the cake for at least 1 hour or up to overnight before serving.

Churro Poke Cake

Churros are a fried pastry traditionally from Mexico or Spain. While many restaurants and bakeries feature them, Kathy's favorite taste was from a food truck that specialized in them, serving the classic cinnamon-sugar ones and others covered with dulce de leche, chocolate, or fruit syrups. That hot, fried pastry was incredible and is forever etched in her food memories. This Churro Poke Cake is not fried, but the cinnamon-sugar sauce makes a crusty sugar layer in the cake that might suggest a crisp, fried churro. Add a layer of dulce de leche, and you have an amazing dessert.

Nonstick cooking spray

1 (15.25- to 18-ounce) box yellow cake mix

Eggs, oil, and water as directed on the cake mix box

6 tablespoons (¾ stick) unsalted butter, melted

⅔ cup packed dark brown sugar

1 tablespoon ground cinnamon, plus more for garnish, if desired

1 (13.4-ounce) can dulce de leche

1 (8-ounce) tub frozen whipped topping, thawed

Preheat the oven to 350°F. Spray a 9 x 13-inch baking dish with nonstick cooking spray.

Prepare and bake the cake according to the package directions for a 9 x 13-inch cake. Place the cake on a wire rack and let cool completely.

Poke holes evenly over the baked cake using a drinking straw.

In a small bowl, stir together the melted butter, brown sugar, and cinnamon. Drizzle the brown sugar mixture evenly over the cake, filling all the holes.

Place the dulce de leche in a 2-cup microwave-safe glass bowl. Microwave on High (100%) power for 20 to 30 seconds, or until the dulce de leche is just warm. Spoon the dulce de leche over the cake, spreading it evenly with a butter knife and filling in the poked holes. Cover and refrigerate the cake for 1 hour.

Frost the cake with the whipped topping. Garnish the cake with a sprinkling of cinnamon, if desired. Cover and refrigerate the cake for at least 1 hour or up to overnight before serving.

TIPS Dulce de leche is a thick, caramel-like sauce especially popular in South America, Central America, and Mexico. *Dulce de leche*, which translates to "sweet milk," is made from milk that cooks so long it becomes thick, sweet, and golden in color. It is now readily available canned or jarred, so it is easy to use in your recipes. Look for it in larger grocery stores, shelved with Latin American foods or with the evaporated milk.

Chocolate Poke Cakes

S'more Poke Brownies

They say birds of a feather flock together, and the same could be said for Kathy and Roxanne. Both were Girl Scouts growing up, and both have girls who became Girl Scouts, too. Laura, Amanda, and Grace all agree that the taste of s'mores and the friendships created around the campfire were some of their best Girl Scout memories. The joy of those fond days is re-created each and every time we bake these brownies. You don't have to be a Girl Scout to take part in the fun. Enjoy!

Nonstick cooking spray

1 (18.3-ounce) box (9 x 13-inch size) chewy fudge brownie mix

Eggs, oil, and water as directed on the brownie mix box

1 (7.5-ounce) jar marshmallow creme

3 tablespoons water

4 (1.55-ounce) milk chocolate candy bars, broken into small pieces

2 cups broken graham crackers

3 cups mini marshmallows

Preheat the oven to 350°F. Spray a 9 x 13-inch baking dish with nonstick cooking spray.

Prepare and bake brownies according to the package directions for a 9 x 13-inch pan of brownies. Place the brownies on a wire rack, but do not allow to cool.

While the brownies are baking, place the marshmallow creme in a microwave-safe glass bowl. Microwave on High (100%) power for 30 seconds. Add the water and stir until smooth.

Poke holes evenly over the baked brownies using the handle of a wooden spoon. Pour the warm marshmallow cream evenly into the holes and over the top of the hot brownies. Scatter the milk chocolate evenly over the warm marshmallow creme. Sprinkle evenly with the graham crackers and mini marshmallows. Let cool completely before serving.

Chocolate-Cola Poke Cake

Adding cola to a chocolate cake batter and then drizzling that cake with a delicious chocolate-and-cola syrup is an unbeatable combination! This cake is moist and bursting with flavor that can't be beat.

Nonstick cooking spray

1 (15.25- to 18-ounce) box chocolate cake mix

Eggs and oil as directed on the cake mix box

1 cup cola-flavored soda (see Tip)

CHOCOLATE-COLA SYRUP:

½ cup (1 stick) unsalted butter

¼ cup unsweetened cocoa powder

½ cup cola-flavored soda

2 cups confectioners' sugar

1 (8-ounce) tub frozen whipped topping, thawed

TIP

If the cake-mix box recommends an amount of water greater than 1 cup, add water to the soda so it equals the amount called for on the cake-mix box.

Preheat the oven to 350°F. Spray a 9 x 13-inch baking dish with nonstick cooking spray.

Prepare the cake mix according to the package directions, substituting the cola-flavored soda for the water called for on the box. Bake according to the package directions for a 9 x 13-inch cake.

Place the cake on a wire rack to cool for 10 minutes.

Poke holes evenly over the baked cake with a drinking straw.

MAKE THE CHOCOLATE-COLA SYRUP: In a small saucepan, melt the butter over low heat. Stir in the cocoa powder. Stir in the soda and cook, stirring continuously, for 1 minute. Remove from the heat. Stir in the confectioners' sugar and whisk until smooth.

Slowly pour the Chocolate-Cola Syrup over the cake and use the tip of a table knife to smooth and fill the holes. Cover and refrigerate the cake for 1 hour.

Frost the cake with the whipped topping. Cover and refrigerate the cake for at least 1 hour or up to overnight before serving.

Pokey Turtle Cake

Who can resist a gooey caramel center? There is a reason there is a decadent chocolate candy with the same name. Baking Pokey Turtle Cake is much easier than making candy. Be prepared to share the recipe: folks will come back for more and more. No leftovers, we promise!

Nonstick cooking spray

1 (15.25- to 18-ounce) dark chocolate fudge cake mix

Eggs, oil, and water as directed on the cake mix box

¼ cup whole milk

1 (14-ounce) package caramels, unwrapped

CHOCOLATE FROSTING (PAGE 146)

1 cup coarsely chopped pecans, toasted

½ cup mini semisweet chocolate chips

Preheat the oven to 350°F. Spray a 9 x 13-inch baking dish with nonstick cooking spray.

Prepare and bake the cake according to the package directions for a 9 x 13-inch cake. Place the cake on a wire rack to cool for 10 minutes.

Poke holes evenly over the baked cake using the handle of a wooden spoon.

While the cake is cooling, place the milk and caramels in a microwave-safe glass bowl. Microwave on High (100%) power in 30-second intervals, stirring well after each, until the caramels are melted and the mixture is smooth, making sure not to overcook the caramels. Pour the caramel mixture into the poked holes in the cake. Let the cake cool completely.

Frost the cake with the Chocolate Frosting. Sprinkle with the pecans and mini chocolate chips.

TIPS

✴ If you're unable to find a chocolate fudge cake mix, substitute another chocolate cake mix, such as devil's food.

✴ In a hurry? Some days we just don't have the patience to unwrap caramels. If you are running short on time, by all means substitute a jar of caramel ice cream topping for the melted caramels. It won't be as thick and decadent, but shhhh! No one will be the wiser.

✴ We like to use chewy caramels. For this recipe, we prefer to use Brach's Caramels, made with real milk.

Chocolate Mousse Poke Cake

Chocolate lovers, unite. What is better than a chocolate cake? How about one that is poked and filled with hot fudge, then topped with a creamy chocolate mousse? Three layers of chocolate: It is a chocoholic's dream comes true!

Nonstick cooking spray

1 (15.25- to 18-ounce) box chocolate cake mix

3 large eggs

1 cup sour cream

½ cup canola or vegetable oil

½ cup water

1 (11.75-ounce) jar hot fudge ice cream topping

1 cup heavy cream

1 (3.9-ounce) box chocolate fudge or chocolate instant pudding mix

2 cups whole milk

Preheat the oven to 350°F. Spray a 9 x 13-inch baking dish with the nonstick cooking spray.

In a large bowl using a handheld mixer on low speed, beat together the cake mix, eggs, sour cream, oil, and water. Scrape down the sides of the bowl well and beat for 2 minutes on medium speed. Spoon the batter into the prepared baking dish.

Bake for 30 to 35 minutes, or until a wooden pick inserted into the center of the cake comes out clean. Place the cake on a wire rack and let cool completely.

Poke holes evenly over the baked cake using the handle of a wooden spoon.

Heat the hot fudge topping in a microwave according to the directions on the jar. Measure ¼ cup of the hot fudge into a small microwave-safe glass cup and set aside for topping. Pour the remaining hot fudge over the cake and spread with the tip of a table knife to cover completely and fill the holes. Let cool for 15 minutes.

In a small, deep bowl using a handheld mixer, beat the cream on low speed until frothy. Increase the speed to medium-high and beat until the cream holds stiff peaks. Set the whipped cream aside.

(continued)

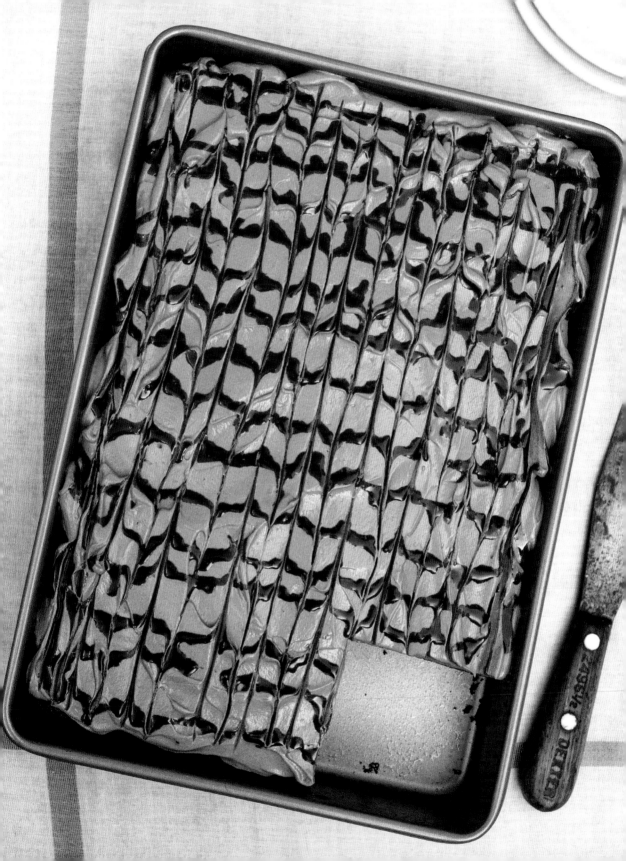

In a medium bowl, whisk together the pudding mix and the milk until the pudding is blended. Fold in the whipped cream.

Spread the mousse over the cake.

Rewarm the reserved hot fudge topping, if necessary, in a microwave on High (100%) power for 5 to 10 seconds, or until just warm. Place small dollops of hot fudge over the top of the mousse. Using a wooden pick, swirl the chocolate dollops to make a decorative pattern.

Cover and refrigerate the cake for at least 1 hour or up to overnight before serving.

Triple Chocolate Brownies

That famous milk chocolate bar from Hershey, Pennsylvania, deserves its own recipe, don't you think? Many of us grew up adoring the special treat of a milk chocolate bar. It was something our parents purchased on very special occasions. Rekindle fond memories of days gone by and make the all-American brownie with the most famous all-American chocolate bar. Add a scoop of vanilla ice cream and drizzle with chocolate syrup by the same iconic name, and you have a million-dollar dessert in our book!

Nonstick cooking spray

1 (18.3-ounce) box
   (9 x 13-inch size) chewy
   fudge brownie mix

Eggs, oil, and water as
   directed on the brownie
   mix box

3 (1.55-ounce) milk chocolate
   candy bars

Chocolate Frosting
   (page 146)

1 cup coarsely chopped
   pecans, toasted, for
   garnish (optional)

Preheat the oven to 350°F. Spray a 9 x 13-inch baking dish with nonstick cooking spray.

Prepare and bake the brownies according to the package directions for a 9 x 13-inch pan of brownies. Place the brownies on a wire rack to cool for only 5 minutes. (This is important, as you do not want the brownies to cool too much.)

Poke 36 holes (four rows across and nine rows down) into the baked brownies using the handle of a wooden spoon. Immediately break the chocolate bars into the rectangles marked on the bar (there are 12 rectangles on each bar). Break each rectangle in half and place both halves in a poked hole in the brownies. Poke as far down as you can; there may be a small amount of chocolate bar sticking out. Let the brownies cool completely.

Frost with the Chocolate Frosting. If desired, sprinkle with the pecans.

Crunchy Toffee Poke Cake

Do you need to bring a dessert to the office party, potluck, or bunko night? No worries! Bake Crunchy Toffee Poke Cake the day ahead, and you've got it covered. This will make the gathering memorable to many, and there won't be one piece left to carry home. That's a good thing, right?

Nonstick cooking spray

1 (15.25- to 18-ounce) German chocolate cake mix

1 (3.9-ounce) box chocolate pudding mix

1 cup sour cream

2/3 cup water

1/2 cup vegetable or canola oil

4 large eggs

1 teaspoon pure vanilla extract

1 (12.25-ounce) jar caramel ice cream topping

1 (8-ounce) tub frozen whipped topping, thawed

4 (1.4-ounce) milk chocolate English toffee candy bars

Preheat the oven to 350°F. Spray a 9 x 13-inch baking dish with nonstick cooking spray.

In a large bowl using a handheld mixer on low speed, beat together the cake mix, pudding mix, sour cream, water, oil, eggs, and vanilla. Scrape down the sides of the bowl well and beat for 2 minutes on medium speed. Pour the batter into the prepared baking dish.

Bake for 30 to 35 minutes, or until a wooden pick inserted into the center of the cake comes out clean. Place the cake on a wire rack to cool for 10 minutes.

Poke holes evenly over the baked cake using the handle of a wooden spoon. Let the cake cool completely.

Drizzle three-quarters of the caramel topping into the holes on the cake. Frost the cake with the whipped topping. Place the candy bars in a zip-top bag and coarsely crush with a rolling pin or mallet. Sprinkle the candy bars evenly over the cake. Refrigerate until ready to serve.

Just before serving, drizzle the top of the cake with the remaining caramel topping.

(continued)

Crunchy Toffee Poke Cake (continued)

VARIATION

You can substitute caramels and milk for the caramel ice-cream topping. Combine 1 (14-ounce) package caramels, unwrapped, and ¼ cup whole milk in a microwave-safe glass bowl. Microwave on High (100%) power in 30-second intervals, stirring well after each, until the caramels are melted and the mixture is smooth, making sure not to overcook the caramels. Pour three-quarters of the caramel mixture into the poked holes in the cake. Warm the remaining caramel mixture in the microwave on high power for 10 to 15 seconds or until warm. Drizzle over the cake just before serving.

 TIP If you want to reduce the amount of chocolate, use a white or yellow cake mix in place of the German chocolate cake mix.

Salted Caramel–Chocolate Poke Cake

A few years ago, most of us in the United States who loved caramel had never thought of adding a flavor punch with salt. While it was a traditional flavor in France, the rest of us didn't have a clue. Finally, a few chefs in the United States started featuring the flavor combo and the rest, as they say, is history. Now salted caramel is everywhere, and it is a popular choice at coffee, ice cream, and candy shops everywhere. Poke cakes cannot be left out, and sure enough, it makes a truly delicious cake.

Nonstick cooking spray

1 (15.25- to 18-ounce) box chocolate cake mix

Eggs, oil, and water as directed on the cake mix box

1 (14-ounce) package caramels, unwrapped

1 (5-ounce) can evaporated milk

½ teaspoon coarsey sea salt, or to taste

Caramel Frosting (page 145)

Preheat the oven to 350°F. Spray a 9 x 13-inch baking dish with nonstick cooking spray.

Prepare and bake the cake according to the package directions for a 9 x 13-inch cake. Place the cake on a wire rack to cool for 10 minutes.

Place the caramels and evaporated milk in a microwave-safe glass bowl. Microwave on High (100%) power in 30-second intervals, stirring well after each, until the caramels are melted and the mixture is smooth, making sure not to overcook the caramels.

Poke holes evenly over the baked cake using the handle of a wooden spoon. Slowly pour the caramel sauce over the cake; use the tip of a table knife to spread the caramel evenly and fill the holes. Sprinkle the caramel layer with the coarse salt. Let the cake cool completely.

Frost the cake with the Caramel Frosting.

 TIPS ❊ Do you prefer a thick layer of luscious caramel frosting? If so, double the Caramel Frosting recipe.

❊ If you prefer, combine the caramels and the evaporated milk in a small saucepan and cook over low heat, stirring frequently, until melted and smooth.

Chocolate-Peanut Butter Poke Cake

It was good—but not over-the-top good. That was the evaluation on the first attempts at making a Chocolate–Peanut Butter Poke Cake. It had to be perfect. So, back to the test kitchen to try again. More cakes and more tastes—someone had to do it for you. You are welcome. We think you will agree that this version is it! The creamy peanut butter permeates the chocolate and is oh so good. Nope, make that great!

Nonstick cooking spray
1 (15.25- to 18-ounce) box chocolate cake mix
1 (3.9-ounce) box chocolate instant pudding mix
4 large eggs
1 cup whole milk
½ cup canola or vegetable oil

PEANUT BUTTER SAUCE:
3 tablespoons unsalted butter
¾ cup creamy peanut butter
½ cup heavy cream
¼ cup confectioners' sugar
2 tablespoons light corn syrup
Chocolate Frosting (page 146)
2 (2.5-ounce) packages unwrapped mini peanut butter cup candies, or 1 cup chopped peanut butter cup candies

Preheat the oven to 350°F. Spray a 9 x 13-inch baking dish with nonstick cooking spray.

In a large bowl using a handheld mixer on low speed, beat together the cake mix, pudding mix, eggs, milk, and oil. Scrape down the sides of the bowl well and beat for 2 minutes on medium speed. Spoon the batter into the prepared baking dish.

Bake for 30 to 35 minutes, or until a wooden pick inserted into the center of the cake comes out clean. Place the cake on a wire rack to cool for 10 minutes.

Poke holes evenly over the baked cake with the handle of a wooden spoon.

MAKE THE PEANUT BUTTER SAUCE: In a small saucepan, heat the butter, peanut butter, and cream over low heat, stirring continuously, until melted and smooth. Remove from the heat and whisk in the confectioners' sugar and corn syrup. Whisk until smooth.

Pour the peanut butter sauce evenly over the cake; use the tip of a table knife to spread the peanut butter sauce evenly and fill the holes. Let the cake cool completely.

Frost the cake with the Chocolate Frosting. Garnish the top of the cake with the peanut butter cup candies.

Chocolate-Chocolate Chip Cookie Poke Cake

Roxanne has a daughter who adores chocolate chip cookies. This recipe for Chocolate-Chocolate Chip Cookie Poke Cake was the answer to her dreams, and she rated it as her all-time favorite of all the poke cake recipes she has taste-tested. You know it's a keeper!

Nonstick cooking spray

1 (1 pound 2.2-ounce) family-size package chocolate chip cookies

1 (15.25- to 18-ounce) box devil's food or chocolate cake mix

Eggs, oil, and water as directed on the cake mix box

1 (3.9-ounce) box chocolate instant pudding mix

2 cups whole milk

1 (8-ounce) tub frozen whipped topping, thawed

3 tablespoons chocolate ice cream syrup

Preheat the oven to 350°F. Spray a 9 x 13-inch baking dish with nonstick cooking spray.

Arrange the chocolate chip cookies in a single layer on the bottom of the prepared baking dish. Break a few cookies, if need be, to cover the entire bottom surface; set aside.

Prepare the cake batter according to the package directions. Pour the batter over the cookies in the baking dish. Bake according to the package directions for a 9 x 13-inch cake.

Place the cake on a wire rack to cool for 25 to 30 minutes.

Poke holes evenly over the baked cake using the handle of a wooden spoon.

In a medium bowl, whisk together the pudding mix and milk until the pudding is blended. Place 14 chocolate chip cookies in a zip-top bag. Using a rolling pin, crush the cookies until they are fine. Add the cookie crumbs to the pudding mixture and blend well.

Pour the pudding mixture evenly over the entire cake, filling the holes. Cover and refrigerate the cake for 1 hour.

Frost the cake with the whipped topping. Coarsely crush or break up the remaining chocolate chip cookies and sprinkle on top of the cake. Drizzle the chocolate ice cream syrup over the entire cake. Refrigerate until ready to serve.

Chocolate Mint Poke Cake

Who doesn't look forward to that time of year when the doorbell rings and your neighborhood Girl Scout asks how many boxes of cookies you would like? At our houses, the Thin Mint variety is the hands-down favorite. Now you can enjoy that flavor all year round.

Nonstick cooking spray

1 (15.25- to 18-ounce) box devil's food or chocolate cake mix

Eggs, oil, and water as directed on the cake mix box

1 (3.9-ounce) box chocolate instant pudding mix

2 cups whole milk

24 thin chocolate-mint wafer cookies

1 (8-ounce) tub frozen whipped topping, thawed

¼ teaspoon peppermint extract

3 or 4 drops green food coloring (optional)

TIP

If you are lucky enough to have Girl Scout Thin Mint cookies, they are excellent in this recipe. If not, we use Keebler brand Grasshopper Cookies.

Preheat the oven to 350°F. Spray a 9 x 13-inch baking dish with nonstick cooking spray.

Prepare and bake the cake according to the package directions for a 9 x 13-inch pan. Place the cake on a wire rack and let cool completely.

Poke holes evenly over the baked cake using the handle of a wooden spoon.

In a medium bowl, whisk together the pudding and milk. Finely crush 12 wafer cookies and stir them into the pudding mixture. Pour evenly over the cake and use the tip of a butter knife to spread the pudding to fill all the holes. Cover and refrigerate for 1 hour.

In a medium bowl, combine the whipped topping, peppermint extract, and food coloring. Stir to blend well. Frost the cake with the whipped topping mixture. Coarsely crush the remaining cookies and sprinkle them over the cake. Cover and refrigerate until ready to serve.

Espresso Brownie Poke

Espresso and chocolate is a match made in heaven, and this Espresso Brownie Poke is over the top! Adding a little espresso powder to a chocolate recipe is a great tip to use anytime as the espresso intensifies the chocolate flavor. This time, espresso is added to a fudge brownie mix, then the brownies are poked and drizzled with a sweetened espresso sauce and, finally, it is frosted with chocolate frosting. It can't get any better, and it's a great afternoon treat in lieu of a cup of java.

Nonstick cooking spray

⅓ cup water plus 2 tablespoons water

½ cup canola or vegetable oil

3 large eggs

2 tablespoons plus 2 teaspoons instant espresso powder

1 (18.3-ounce) box (9 x 13-inch size) chewy fudge brownie mix

⅔ cup semisweet chocolate chips

½ teaspoon pure vanilla extract

1½ cups confectioners' sugar

1 tablespoon unsalted butter, melted

Chocolate Frosting (page 146)

Preheat the oven to 350°F. Spray a 9 x 13-inch baking dish with nonstick cooking spray.

In a large bowl, stir together ⅓ cup of the water, the oil, eggs, and 2 tablespoons of the espresso powder. Add the brownie mix and stir until well blended. Stir in the chocolate chips. Pour into the prepared baking dish. Bake for 20 to 25 minutes, or until a wooden pick inserted into the center comes out with a few crumbs attached. Place the brownies on a wire rack and let cool completely.

Poke holes evenly over the baked cake using the handle of a wooden spoon.

In a small bowl, stir together the remaining 2 teaspoons espresso powder and the remaining 2 tablespoons water. Whisk in the vanilla extract, confectioners' sugar, and butter. Pour over the holes in the brownies, using a butter knife to spread the glaze evenly over the entire surface of the brownie. Let cool completely.

Frost with Chocolate Frosting.

 TIP For a fun presentation, cut the brownies into squares. Place a chocolate-covered espresso bean in the center of each square.

Favorite Cookie Poke Cake

If you deconstruct those iconic cookies into parts, you'll find a chocolate base and a layer of creamy vanilla filling, and that sounds like a perfect flavor combo for a poke cake. Crushed cookies on the top of this cake are the finishing touch!

Nonstick cooking spray

1 (15.25- to 18-ounce) box dark chocolate fudge or devil's food cake mix

Eggs, oil, and water as directed on the cake mix box

1 (3.4-ounce) box vanilla instant pudding mix

1¾ cups whole milk

1⅓ cups vanilla cream–filled chocolate sandwich cookie crumbs (17 or 18 cookies, finely crushed)

1 (8-ounce) tub frozen whipped topping, thawed

TIP

To make the fine cookie crumbs, place the cookies in a zip-top bag. Using a rolling pin, crush the cookies until they are fine.

Preheat the oven to 350°F. Spray a 9 x 13-inch baking dish with nonstick cooking spray.

Prepare and bake the cake according to the package directions for a 9 x 13-inch cake. Place the cake on a wire rack and let cool completely.

Poke holes evenly over the baked cake using the handle of a wooden spoon.

In a medium bowl, whisk together the pudding mix and the milk until the pudding is blended. Stir ⅓ cup of the cookie crumbs into the pudding. Pour the pudding mixture over the cake, spreading it evenly and filling in the poked holes. Cover and refrigerate the cake for 1 hour. Seal the remaining cookie crumbs in a zip-top bag and set aside.

Frost the cake with the whipped topping. Cover and refrigerate the cake for at least 1 hour or up to overnight.

Sprinkle the remaining cookie crumbs over the top of the cake just before serving.

Coconut Caramel Poke Cake

This cake has nothing at all to do with the Polynesian island of Samoa and everything to do with a fantastic Girl Scout cookie. Depending on the part of the country you live in, and hence the bakery that your Girl Scout council uses, you either know these cookies as Samoas or Caramel deLites. Either way, the tasty cookie is enrobed in caramel, toasted coconut, and chocolate. We were Girl Scouts, and our daughters were Girl Scouts, too, so we support the Scouts and buy lots of these cookies. But between cookie seasons, why not make this delightful Coconut Caramel Poke Cake? We love it and promise you will love it, too.

Nonstick cooking spray
1 (15.25- to 18-ounce) devil's
food cake mix
Eggs, oil, and water as
directed on the cake mix
box
1½ cups caramel ice cream
topping
1 (7-ounce) bag sweetened
shredded or flaked
coconut, toasted
⅓ cup chocolate fudge ice
cream topping

Toasted coconut has a more
intense flavor. To toast coconut, preheat the oven to 350°F.
Spread coconut evenly on a
rimmed baking sheet.
Bake, stirring occasionally, for
7 to 8 minutes or until light
golden brown.

Preheat the oven to 350°F. Spray a 9 x 13-inch baking dish with nonstick cooking spray.

Prepare and bake the cake according to the package directions for a 9 x 13-inch cake. Place the cake on a wire rack and let cool completely.

Poke holes evenly over the baked cake using a drinking straw.

Drizzle ½ cup of the caramel over the cake, filling all the holes.

In a medium bowl, stir together the toasted coconut and the remaining 1 cup caramel. Stir until the coconut is evenly covered in the caramel. Spoon the coconut mixture evenly over the cake, then use the tip of a butter knife to gently spread the coconut to cover the cake evenly.

Place the chocolate fudge ice cream topping in a small microwave-safe glass bowl. Microwave on High (100%) power for 15 seconds, or until the fudge is just warm. Pour the warm fudge into a small zip-top bag. Clip off the corner of the bag. Drizzle the chocolate fudge in thin stripes over the coconut.

Candy Bar Joy Poke Cake

Who doesn't love that iconic candy bar that has coconut enrobed in milk chocolate with an almond on top? Now, if you bake this Candy Bar Joy Poke Cake, you can share that incredible flavor with those you love, and you can even enjoy seconds and thirds any time you please!

Nonstick cooking spray

1 (15.25- to 18-ounce) box devil's food or chocolate cake mix

Eggs, oil, and water as directed on the cake mix box

1 (14-ounce) can sweetened condensed milk

2 cups sweetened shredded or flaked coconut

2 cups semisweet chocolate chips

⅓ cup (5⅓ tablespoons) unsalted butter, cut into small pieces

3 tablespoons whole milk

⅓ cup sliced almonds, toasted

TIP

Toasting the almonds intensifies their flavor. Follow the directions on page 8 as to how to toast the nuts.

Preheat the oven to 350°F. Spray a 9 x 13-inch baking dish with nonstick cooking spray.

Prepare and bake the cake according to the package directions for a 9 x 13-inch pan. Place the cake on a wire rack to cool for 20 minutes.

Poke holes evenly over the baked cake using the handle of a wooden spoon.

In a medium bowl, combine the sweetened condensed milk and coconut; stir to blend well. Spoon the coconut mixture over the baked cake, filling the holes and spreading the mixture evenly.

Place the chocolate chips, butter, and milk in a microwave-safe glass bowl. Microwave on High (100%) power in 30-second increments, stirring well after each 30 seconds. Do this until the mixture is melted and smooth. (This should take no more than about 1 minute.) Do not over-microwave. Pour over the coconut layer and spread to cover the entire cake. Sprinkle with almonds.

French Silk Poke Cake

French silk pie is not French, but the rich and silky chocolate mousse filling is scrumptious. Pillsbury lists it as a winning recipe in their famous Bake-Off in 1951, and it has been popular ever since. Many restaurants and bakeries make a signature French silk pie, and when Tippin's opened their restaurant in Kansas City, they became famous for their French silk pie. This French Silk Poke Cake captures the rich chocolate flavor but still keeps the light, mousse-like filling. One little ripple in its tasty history is that the original recipe featured uncooked eggs. No worries, for we developed the perfect mousse filling, without the eggs, then used it to top a chocolate cake.

Nonstick cooking spray
1 (15.25- to 18-ounce) milk chocolate or devil's food cake mix
Eggs, oil, and water as directed on the cake mix box
1 (5.9-ounce) box chocolate instant pudding mix
2 cups whole milk
½ cup sour cream
1 (12-ounce) large tub frozen whipped topping, thawed
Chocolate curls, for garnish

Preheat the oven to 350°F. Spray a 9 x 13-inch baking dish with nonstick cooking spray.

Prepare and bake the cake according to the package directions for a 9 x 13-inch cake. Place the cake on a wire rack and let cool completely.

Poke holes evenly over the baked cake using a drinking straw.

In a medium bowl, whisk together the pudding mix, the milk, and the sour cream until the pudding is blended. Gently stir in 2 cups of the whipped topping. Immediately spoon the pudding mixture over the cake, spreading it to fill the holes. Cover and refrigerate for 1 hour. Cover and refrigerate the remaining whipped topping.

Frost the cake with the remaining whipped topping. Garnish the top of the cake with chocolate curls.

 TIPS

❊ To easily make chocolate curls, use a vegetable peeler to peel thin strips of chocolate off a milk chocolate candy bar.

❊ The frozen whipped topping carton used in this recipe is the larger, 12-ounce tub. If not available, substitute 1½ (8-ounce) tubs.

Chocolate and Vanilla Poke 'n' Tote Cakes

Neat and portable, these luscious chocolate cakes are ready to take to the park, soccer field, or office, or any time you want a dessert to go. They are a winner, and the chocolate cake, topped with a creamy vanilla pudding and then a chocolate glaze, just may remind you of a cream-filled snack cake!

Nonstick cooking spray

½ cup boiling water

⅓ cup unsweetened cocoa powder

1 cup all-purpose flour

1 cup sugar

1 teaspoon baking powder

¾ teaspoon baking soda

⅛ teaspoon salt

1 large egg

2½ cups whole milk

⅓ cup canola or vegetable oil

1 teaspoon pure vanilla extract

1 (3.4-ounce) box vanilla instant pudding mix

CHOCOLATE GLAZE

4 tablespoons (½ stick) unsalted butter, cut into pieces

⅓ cup unsweetened cocoa powder

1 cup confectioners' sugar

2½ tablespoons whole milk

½ teaspoon pure vanilla extract

Preheat the oven to 350°F. Spray 12 (8-ounce) canning jars with nonstick cooking spray. Set the lids and rings aside.

In a small bowl, whisk together the boiling water and cocoa powder until smooth; set aside.

In a large bowl, whisk together the flour, sugar, baking powder, baking soda, and salt. Using a handheld mixer on low speed, beat in the egg, ½ cup of the milk, the oil, vanilla, and cocoa mixture. Scrape down the sides of the bowl well and beat for 2 minutes on medium speed. Spoon about ¼ cup of the batter into each prepared jar. Do not cover.

Arrange the jars in a shallow baking pan, leaving about 1 inch between the jars. Bake for 24 to 28 minutes, or until a wooden pick inserted into the center of the cakes comes out clean. (Do not overbake.) Place the baking pan with the jars in it on a wire rack and let the cakes cool completely.

Poke holes evenly over the baked cakes in the jars using a drinking straw.

In a medium bowl, whisk together the pudding mix and the remaining 2 cups of milk until the pudding is blended. Spoon about 2 tablespoons of the pudding over each cake. Seal each jar with its lid and ring and refrigerate the cakes for 1 hour.

(continued)

TIPS

❋ Use caution when testing the cake for doneness or removing the pan of jars from the oven as the jars will be hot.

❋ Pack the Poke 'n' Tote Cakes in a cooler with ice packs to transport to a park or other outside event. Use ribbon or string to tie a plastic spoon to each jar.

MAKE THE CHOCOLATE GLAZE: In a small saucepan, melt the butter over low heat. Stir in the cocoa powder. Remove from the heat. Stir in the confectioners' sugar until smooth. Add the milk and vanilla and stir until smooth. The glaze should be thin enough to drizzle off the tip of a spoon.

Spoon about 1 tablespoon of the Chocolate Glaze over the pudding in each jar. Gently, using the back of a spoon, spread the glaze to cover the pudding completely. Seal each jar again and refrigerate for at least 1 hour or up to overnight before serving.

VARIATIONS

Poke Cupcakes: Line muffin pans with paper liners. Prepare the batter as directed and spoon it into the prepared pan, filling each cup about halfway full. Bake 15 to 18 minutes, or until a wooden pick inserted into the center of the cakes comes out clean. Proceed as the recipe directs, poking the cakes with a drinking straw, topping with pudding, and spreading the pudding to the edge of the cupcakes. Top with the glaze, gently covering the pudding.

Individual Poke Cakes: Instead of canning jars, prepare the individual poke cakes in 8-ounce ovenproof ramekins. Spray the ramekins with nonstick cooking spray, then spoon in the batter, filling ramekins about halfway. Bake for 15 to 18 minutes, or until a wooden pick inserted into the center of the cakes comes out clean. Proceed as the recipe directs, poking the cakes with a drinking straw, topping with pudding, and spreading the pudding to the edge of the cakes. Top with the glaze, gently covering the pudding.

Flavorful Fruit Poke Cakes

Strawberry Shortcake Poke Cake

Baking is fun, and on some days can resemble child's play. Why not let your little ones take pride in preparing scrumptious Strawberry Shortcake Poke Cake for that special summer occasion? The recipe comes together in a snap, yet is elegant enough for the most glamorous party.

1 (16-ounce) package family-size frozen pound cake, thawed

1 cup water

1 (3-ounce) box strawberry gelatin

1 cup frozen sliced strawberries in syrup, thawed

½ (8-ounce) tub frozen whipped topping, thawed

1½ to 2 cups fresh strawberries

TIPS

❋ For a colorful presentation, use a variety of berries for garnishing, such as blueberries, blackberries, raspberries, and strawberries.

❋ Substitute sweetened whipped cream for the frozen whipped topping.

Carefully remove the lid from the pound cake and save the lid. (Leave the pound cake in the foil container.) Poke holes evenly over the cake using a drinking straw, poking through to the bottom of the cake.

Place the water in a 4-cup microwave-safe glass bowl. Microwave on High (100%) power for 2 to 3 minutes, or until the water comes to a boil. Stir the gelatin into the water until dissolved.

Place the strawberries with the syrup in a blender or food processor. Process until the mixture is smooth. Pour the strawberry puree into the gelatin mixture and stir to blend well. Pour the gelatin mixture into the holes in the pound cake slowly, allowing time for the mixture to soak through. Place the lid on the pound cake and refrigerate overnight.

Remove the lid from the pound cake. Using kitchen scissors, carefully cut the foil pound cake container at the four corners. Carefully peel away the container and invert the pound cake onto a cake plate. Frost the pound cake with the whipped topping, frosting just the top or the top and sides as you prefer. Leave the strawberries whole or slice them thickly and layer them around the bottom and top of the shortcake. Refrigerate until ready to serve.

Cherry-Almond Poke Cake

Roxanne's daughter, Grace, almost always chooses chocolate cake—that is, until she taste-tested Cherry Almond Poke Cake. She gave this recipe "two thumbs up" and wanted to make sure that Roxanne did not give any samples away to neighbors or friends. This is how the recipe made it into the "permanent, must make again" recipe file.

Nonstick cooking spray

1 (15.25- to 18-ounce) box cherry chip cake mix

Eggs, oil, and water as directed on the cake mix box

1 teaspoon pure almond extract

1 cup water

1 (3-ounce) box cherry gelatin

½ cup cold water

1 (8-ounce) tub frozen whipped topping, thawed

TIPS

✳ If desired, garnish the top of the cake with maraschino cherry halves that have been drained and patted dry with paper towels.

✳ If desired, use a white cake mix in place of the cherry chip cake mix.

Preheat the oven to 350°F. Spray a 9 x 13-inch baking dish with nonstick cooking spray; set aside.

Prepare the cake batter according to the package directions. Stir ½ teaspoon of the almond extract into the batter. Bake according to the package directions for a 9 x 13-inch cake.

Place the cake on a wire rack to cool for 10 minutes.

Poke holes evenly over the baked cake using a drinking straw.

Place the 1 cup water in a 4-cup microwave-safe glass bowl. Microwave on High (100%) power for 2 to 3 minutes, or until the water comes to a boil. Stir the gelatin into the water until it is dissolved. Stir in the ½ cup cold water. Pour the gelatin mixture evenly over the cake. Cover and refrigerate the cake for 1 hour.

Stir the remaining ½ teaspoon almond extract into the whipped topping. Frost the cake with the whipped topping. Cover and refrigerate the cake for at least 1 hour or up to overnight before serving.

Key Lime Poke Cake

This cake is so tasty that Jimmy Buffet is sure to write a tropical song about it! If you can't make it to Margaritaville this week, why not bake up the next best thing? If fresh key limes aren't available, please don't let that stop you. Use bottled key lime juice or substitute supermarket limes and enjoy.

Nonstick cooking spray
1 (15.25- to 18-ounce) box
    lemon supreme cake mix
1 (3-ounce) box lime gelatin
3 large eggs
1 cup water
⅓ cup canola or vegetable
    oil

GLAZE:
1 teaspoon grated lime zest
¼ cup confectioners' sugar
¼ cup fresh lime juice
¼ cup fresh key lime juice

Lime Cream Cheese Frosting
    (page 143)
Grated lime zest, for garnish
    (optional)

Preheat the oven to 350°F. Spray a 9 x 13-inch baking dish with nonstick cooking spray.

In a large bowl using a handheld mixer on low speed, beat together the cake mix, gelatin, eggs, water, and oil. Scrape down the sides of the bowl well and beat for 2 minutes on medium speed. Pour the batter into the prepared baking dish.

Bake for 25 to 30 minutes, or until a wooden pick inserted into the center of the cake comes out clean.

Place the cake on a wire rack. Poke holes evenly over the baked cake using the tines of a fork.

MAKE THE GLAZE: In a small bowl, combine the lime zest, confectioners' sugar, lime juice, and key lime juice and stir until blended. While the cake is still warm, pour the glaze over the cake. Allow the cake to cool completely.

Frost the cake with the Lime Cream Cheese Frosting. If desired, garnish the frosting with additional grated lime zest. Refrigerate until ready to serve.

 Key limes are smaller and not quite as tart as Persian limes, the typical limes found in the grocery store. If key limes are not available, substitute an equal quantity of fresh Persian lime juice. In a pinch, you could substitute bottled key lime juice, but we always prefer the flavor of fresh when possible.

Pink Lemonade Poke Cake

Imagine a refreshing sip of ice-cold lemonade on a hot day. Just sit back and let the cold, sweet-tart thirst quencher take over. The flavor is "just right," and nothing else, even the heat of the day, matters. That is the power of lemonade, and if you love it as much as we do, then Pink Lemonade Poke Cake is the cake to serve. There is just no comparison!

Nonstick cooking spray

1 (15.25- to 18-ounce) box white cake mix

Eggs, oil, and water as directed on the cake mix box

1 cup water

1 (3-ounce) box lemon gelatin

¾ cup frozen pink lemonade concentrate, thawed

1 or 2 drops red food coloring (optional)

PINK LEMONADE FROSTING:

½ cup (1 stick) unsalted butter, softened

4 cups confectioners' sugar

5 tablespoons frozen pink lemonade concentrate, thawed, plus more if needed

1 or 2 drops red food coloring (optional)

Preheat the oven to 350°F. Spray a 9 x 13-inch baking dish with nonstick cooking spray.

Prepare and bake the cake according to the package directions for a 9 x 13-inch cake. Place the cake on a wire rack to cool for 10 minutes.

Place the water in a 4-cup microwave-safe glass bowl. Microwave on High (100 %) power for 2 to 3 minutes, or until the water comes to a boil. Stir the gelatin into the water until dissolved. Stir in the lemonade concentrate until combined. Stir in the red food coloring, if desired.

Poke holes evenly over the baked cake using the tines of a fork. Slowly pour the lemon mixture over the cake, allowing it to seep into the holes. Cover and refrigerate the cake for 1 hour.

MAKE THE PINK LEMONADE FROSTING: In a medium bowl using a handheld mixer, beat the butter on medium-high speed until creamy. Add the confectioners' sugar and lemonade concentrate and beat until light and creamy. (Add an additional tablespoon of lemonade concentrate if a softer frosting is desired.) Add the red food coloring, if desired.

Frost the cake with the Pink Lemonade Frosting. Refrigerate until ready to serve.

(continued)

Pink Lemonade Poke Cake (continued)

 TIP Pink or yellow? Both lemonades taste great. We used pink lemonade, as it contrasted beautifully with the white cake, but you can substitute yellow frozen lemonade concentrate for the pink if you desire. If you do, omit the red food coloring.

Hawaiian Pineapple Poke Cake

A trip to Hawaii is a dream come true: the beautiful beaches, ocean breezes, palm trees, and flowers—and, of course, the food. Pineapple as sweet as candy and coconut like none you have tasted anywhere else are memorable. The good news is, you don't have to be on the island, nor have even traveled to this glorious state, to enjoy this cake. One taste, and if you shut your eyes, you just might feel those oceans waves tickling your toes.

Nonstick cooking spray

1 (15.25- to 18-ounce) box yellow cake mix

Eggs, oil, and water as directed on the cake mix box

PINEAPPLE TOPPING:

2 (8-ounce) cans crushed pineapple in juice, not drained

4 teaspoons cornstarch

2 tablespoons unsalted butter, cut into ½-inch pieces

¼ cup packed dark brown sugar

1 (8-ounce) tub frozen whipped topping, thawed

¾ cup sweetened flaked coconut, toasted

½ cup dry-roasted unsalted macadamia nuts, chopped and toasted (optional)

Preheat the oven to 350°F. Spray a 9 x 13-inch dish with nonstick cooking spray.

Prepare and bake the cake according to the package directions for a 9 x 13-inch cake. Place the cake on a wire rack and let cool completely.

Poke holes evenly over the baked cake using the handle of a wooden spoon.

MAKE THE PINEAPPLE TOPPING: In a small saucepan, stir together the pineapple with the juice and the cornstarch. Stir in the butter and brown sugar. Cook over medium heat, stirring continuously, until boiling. Continue cooking, stirring continuously, until thickened and bubbling. Spoon the mixture evenly over the cake and use the back of a spoon to spread it evenly and fill the holes. Cover and refrigerate the cake for 1 hour.

Frost the cake with the whipped topping. Cover and refrigerate the cake for at least 1 hour or up to overnight before serving.

Just before serving, sprinkle the coconut and nuts (if using) evenly over the cake.

 TIPS

✳ Toasted coconut has a more intense flavor. To toast coconut, preheat the oven to 350°F. Spread coconut evenly over a rimmed baking sheet. Bake, stirring occasionally, for 7 to 8 minutes, or until light golden brown. Let cool completely before sprinkling on the cake.

Strawberry Rhubarb Poke Cake

Strawberry and rhubarb, together forever. One without the other just seems lonely. The sweet-and-sour combination begs for forgiveness with the addition of sweetened whipped cream as a garnish. There! You've created a baking experience of pure nirvana.

Nonstick cooking spray

1 (16-ounce) package frozen sliced rhubarb

½ cup sugar

1 (15.25- to 18-ounce) vanilla or white cake mix

Eggs, oil, and water as directed on the cake mix box

1 cup water

1 (3-ounce) box strawberry gelatin

½ cup cold water

1 cup heavy cream

2 tablespoons confectioners' sugar

Fresh strawberries, sliced, for garnish (optional)

TIP

Substitute 1 (8-ounce) tub frozen whipped topping, thawed, for the sweetened whipped cream. Frost as directed.

Preheat the oven to 350°F. Spray a 9 x 13-inch baking dish with nonstick cooking spray.

Arrange the rhubarb evenly over the bottom of the prepared dish. Sprinkle evenly with the sugar.

Prepare the cake batter according to the package directions. Pour the batter over the rhubarb and sugar in the baking dish. Bake according to the package directions for a 9 x 13-inch cake.

Place the cake on a wire rack to cool for 10 minutes.

Poke holes evenly over the baked cake using the tines of a fork.

Place the 1 cup water in a 4-cup microwave-safe glass bowl. Microwave on High (100%) power for 2 to 3 minutes, or until the water comes to a boil. Stir the gelatin into the water until it is dissolved. Stir in the ½ cup cold water. Pour the gelatin mixture evenly over the cake. Cover and refrigerate the cake for 1 hour.

In a medium bowl using a handheld mixer, beat the cream and confectioners' sugar on medium-high speed until the cream holds stiff peaks.

Frost the cake with the whipped cream. Refrigerate until ready to serve.

If desired, place sliced fresh strawberries on top of the whipped cream.

Carrot Cake Poke Cake

Rich and chock-full of not only carrots, but often pineapple, pecans, and raisins, and then topped with cream cheese frosting, carrot cake is one of the grandes dames of cakes. Many people list it as their favorite cake flavor, but since they think it is hard to make, they only enjoy it when eating out. This delicious Carrot Cake Poke Cake is wonderful, but it is absolutely no stress! It is so easy, you have to try it for yourself.

Nonstick cooking spray

1 (15.25- to 18-ounce) box carrot cake mix

Eggs, oil, and water as directed on the cake mix box

1 (8-ounce) can crushed pineapple in juice, well drained

½ cup chopped pecans, toasted, plus more, if desired, for garnish

⅓ cup raisins

1 (3.4-ounce) box cheesecake or vanilla instant pudding mix

2 cups whole milk

2 tablespoons minced crystallized ginger (optional)

Cream Cheese Frosting (page 143)

Preheat the oven to 350°F. Spray a 9 x 13-inch baking dish with nonstick cooking spray.

Prepare the cake batter according to the package directions. Stir in the crushed pineapple, pecans, and raisins. Pour the batter into the prepared baking dish.

Bake for 30 to 35 minutes, or until a wooden pick inserted into the center of the cake comes out clean. Place the cake on a wire rack and let cool completely.

Poke holes evenly over the baked cake using the handle of a wooden spoon.

In a medium bowl, whisk together the pudding mix and the milk until the pudding is blended. Stir in the ginger, if desired. Immediately pour the pudding mixture over the cake. Use the tip of a table knife to spread the pudding evenly, filling the holes. Cover and refrigerate the cake for 1 hour.

Frost the cake with the Cream Cheese Frosting. Garnish with additional pecans, if desired. Refrigerate until ready to serve.

 TIPS

❈ To drain the pineapple, pour the fruit into a strainer set over a bowl and press lightly on the fruit with the back of a spoon. Reserved juice can be substituted for an equal amount of water when preparing the cake mix. (Be sure to add water as needed to equal the amount of water required by the mix.)

❈ Crystallized ginger, sometimes called candied ginger, is delicious. The chewy pieces are easily chopped with a sharp knife. Look for bottles in the grocery store near spices and herbs.

Orange Cream Poke Cake

The bells on the ice cream truck ring out happily as it meanders up and down the neighborhood streets and kids of all ages run to the corner. Is there any sound as joyful and inviting as the ice cream truck? You instantly know that summer fun and tasty treats are on their way. What is your favorite flavor? Could it be an Orange Creamsicle? Don't wait for the truck to come by, for you can combine those fresh flavors in this delicious Orange Cream Poke Cake.

Nonstick cooking spray

1 (15.25- to 18-ounce) box white cake mix

3 large eggs

1 cup sour cream

½ cup whole milk

¼ cup oil

1 cup orange sherbet

1 cup water

1 (3-ounce) box orange gelatin

VANILLA TOPPING

1 (3.4-ounce) box vanilla instant pudding mix

1½ cups whole milk

1 teaspoon pure vanilla extract

1 (8-ounce) tub frozen whipped topping, thawed

Preheat the oven to 350°F. Spray a 9 x 13-inch baking dish with nonstick cooking spray.

In a large bowl using a handheld mixer on low speed, blend together the cake mix, eggs, sour cream, milk, and oil. Scrape down the sides of the bowl well and beat for 2 minutes on medium speed. Pour the batter into the prepared baking dish.

Bake for 30 to 35 minutes, or until a wooden pick inserted into the center of the cake comes out clean. Place the cake on a wire rack to cool for 15 minutes.

Remove the sherbet from the freezer and allow to soften for 15 minutes at room temperature.

Poke holes evenly over the baked cake using a drinking straw.

Place the water in a 4-cup microwave-safe glass bowl. Microwave on High (100%) power for 2 to 3 minutes, or until the water comes to a boil. Stir the gelatin into the water until it is dissolved. Add the sherbet and stir until the sherbet has melted and the liquid is blended and smooth. Slowly pour the gelatin mixture over the cake and allow it to seep into the cake. Cover and refrigerate the cake for 1 hour.

MAKE THE VANILLA TOPPING: In a medium bowl, whisk together the pudding and the milk until the pudding is blended. Stir in the vanilla. Fold in the whipped topping.

Frost the cake with the Vanilla Topping. Cover and refrigerate the cake for at least 1 hour or up to overnight before serving.

Sticky Toffee–Date Poke Cake

The inspiration for Sticky Toffee–Date Poke Cake comes from the delicious sticky toffee pudding that is especially popular in Great Britain. In England, a pudding is more like a cake, and both the famous pudding and this poke cake are chock-full of chopped dates and topped with a toffee sauce. The toffee sauce is a sweet topping, so there is no need for frosting. Just serve pieces with a dollop of whipped cream.

Nonstick cooking spray

1 (6-ounce) package chopped pitted dates (1½ cups)

⅔ cup boiling water

1 (15.25- to 18-ounce) box yellow cake mix

1 (3.4-ounce) box butterscotch instant pudding mix

4 large eggs

⅔ cup sour cream

½ cup canola or vegetable oil

TOFFEE SAUCE:

6 tablespoons (3/4 stick) unsalted butter, cut into 1-tablespoon pieces

1 cup packed dark brown sugar

½ cup heavy cream

Sweetened whipped cream or frozen whipped topping, thawed

Preheat the oven to 350°F. Spray a 9 x 13-inch baking dish with nonstick cooking spray.

In a large bowl, combine the dates and the boiling water. Let stand for 5 minutes. Do not drain.

Add the cake mix, pudding mix, eggs, sour cream, and oil to the bowl with the dates. Using a handheld mixer on low speed, beat until blended. Scrape down the sides of the bowl well and beat for 2 minutes on medium speed. Pour the batter into the prepared baking dish.

Bake for 40 to 45 minutes, or until a wooden pick inserted into the center of the cake comes out clean. Place the cake on a wire rack and let cool completely.

MAKE THE TOFFEE SAUCE: In a small saucepan, heat the butter, brown sugar, and heavy cream over medium-low heat, stirring frequently, until the butter melts. Cook, stirring frequently, until the mixture comes to a rolling boil. Boil for 3 minutes. Remove from the heat and let cool for 5 minutes.

Poke holes evenly over the baked cake using the tines of a fork. Slowly and evenly pour the warm toffee sauce over the cake. Let stand for 30 minutes before serving.

Serve pieces of the cake with a dollop of the whipped cream or whipped topping.

Down-South Banana Pudding Poke Cake

Babies who grew up in the South admit to being weaned from milk straight to banana pudding. No self-respecting Southerner ever made banana pudding without vanilla wafer cookies. Now you can have your cake, cookies, and pudding, too!

Nonstick cooking spray

1 (15.25- to 18-ounce) yellow cake mix

Eggs, oil, and water as directed on the cake mix box

35 vanilla wafer cookies

2 (3.4-ounce) boxes banana cream instant pudding mix

3 cups whole milk

1 (8-ounce) tub frozen whipped topping, thawed

3 or 4 bananas, sliced

Crushed vanilla wafers, for garnish (optional)

 TIPS

* If making ahead, prepare the recipe through the frosting with the whipped topping. Cover with plastic wrap and refrigerate until ready to serve. Frost and top with sliced bananas just before serving.

* If desired, omit the vanilla wafers and proceed as directed. After topping the cake with the sliced bananas, sprinkle with about ¾ cup graham cracker crumbs.

Preheat the oven to 350°F. Spray a 9 x 13-inch baking dish with nonstick cooking spray.

Prepare the cake batter according to the package directions. Pour about ½ to 1 cup of the batter into the prepared dish and smooth to cover the dish evenly. Set the remaining batter aside.

Arrange the vanilla wafers in the cake batter in the dish, arranging them in evenly in five rows across and seven rows down.

Pour the remaining batter over the cookies in the baking dish. Bake according to the package directions for a 9 x 13-inch cake.

Place the cake on a wire rack to cool for 10 minutes.

Poke holes evenly over the baked cake using the handle of a wooden spoon.

In a medium bowl, whisk together the pudding mix and the milk until the pudding is blended. Pour the pudding mixture over the cake, filling the holes. Cover and refrigerate the cake for 1 hour.

Frost the cake with the whipped topping and top with the sliced bananas. Serve immediately.

If desired, garnish the top of the cake with crushed vanilla wafers.

(continued)

Cherry Vanilla Ice Cream Poke Cake

There is a specialty ice cream/hamburger chain in the southeast that serves cherry pecan ice cream. Roxanne loves to go on working road trips so that we can stop and order a cherry milk shake as a special treat. We really are friends and spend the travel time talking, laughing, and planning! One year for Roxanne's birthday, Kathy had 4 gallons of her favorite ice cream delivered to Roxanne. It was a birthday to remember! When developing recipes for this book, it was fun to create a poke cake with those same flavors. This Cherry Vanilla Ice Cream Poke Cake is for you, Roxanne!

Nonstick cooking spray

1 (15.25- to 18-ounce) box vanilla or white cake mix

Eggs, oil, and water as directed on the cake mix box

2 cups cherry vanilla ice cream, melted

1 (8-ounce) tub frozen whipped topping, thawed

3 tablespoons chocolate ice cream syrup

1 to 2 tablespoons multicolored sprinkles or jimmies

12 to 16 maraschino cherries, stemmed and well drained

Preheat the oven to 350°F. Spray a 9 x 13-inch baking dish with nonstick cooking spray.

Prepare and bake the cake according to the package directions for a 9 x 13-inch cake. Place the cake on a wire rack and let cool completely.

Poke holes evenly over the baked cake using the handle of a wooden spoon.

Pour the melted ice cream into the holes and evenly over the cake. Cover and refrigerate for 1 hour.

Frost the cake with the whipped topping. Drizzle with chocolate ice cream syrup and sprinkle with sprinkles. Place drained cherries evenly on the cake. Refrigerate until ready to serve.

VARIATION: ICE CREAM POKE CAKE

Use any of your favorite flavors of melted ice cream in place of cherry vanilla. Proceed as directed.

Burst of Lemon Poke Cake

For this Burst of Lemon Poke Cake, the fresh lemon juice drizzle on the white cake creates an ideal balance of sweet and tart. It is just that perfect pop of flavor that delights. Serve this poke cake any time of year, but we especially love to serve lemon desserts in the spring, when that fresh flavor seems perfect for the season.

Nonstick cooking spray

1 (15.25- to 18-ounce) box white cake mix

Eggs, oil, and water as directed on the cake mix box

Grated zest of 1 lemon

1/3 cup fresh lemon juice

1 2/3 cups confectioners' sugar

1 tablespoon unsalted butter, melted

1 (3.4-ounce) box lemon instant pudding mix

1 3/4 cups whole milk

1 (8-ounce) tub frozen whipped topping, thawed

TIP

If desired, garnish the cake with lemon twists. To do this, very thinly slice a lemon. Using the tip of a sharp knife, cut from the edge of the slice into the center. Twist and arrange on the cake.

Preheat the oven to 350°F. Spray a 9 x 13-inch baking dish with nonstick cooking spray.

Prepare and bake the cake according to the package directions for a 9 x 13-inch cake. Place the cake on a wire rack and let cool completely.

Poke holes evenly over the baked cake using a drinking straw.

In a small bowl, stir together the lemon zest, lemon juice, confectioners' sugar, and melted butter. Whisk until smooth.

Pour the lemon juice mixture evenly over the cake, filling all the holes. Cover and refrigerate the cake for 1 hour.

In a medium bowl, whisk together the pudding mix and the milk until the pudding is blended. Pour the pudding over the top of the cake, spreading it evenly and filling in the holes. Cover and refrigerate the cake for 1 hour.

Frost the cake with the whipped topping. Cover and refrigerate the cake for at least 1 hour or up to overnight before serving.

Triple Berry Poke Cake

Triple berries, a beautiful combination of strawberries, raspberries, and blueber-
ries, is idyllic summer fare. Sweet and juicy, this combo is sublime and those same
flavors are the stars of this Triple Berry Poke Cake. Garnish the cake with an array
of fresh berries, and it will be just as pretty as it is delicious.

Nonstick cooking spray

1 (15.25- to 18-ounce) box
strawberry cake mix

Eggs, oil, and water as
directed on the cake mix
box

¼ cup blueberry jam

1 cup water

1 (3-ounce) box raspberry
gelatin

½ cup cold water

1 (8-ounce) tub frozen
whipped topping, thawed

Fresh sliced strawberries,
raspberries, and
blueberries, for garnish

Preheat the oven to 350°F. Spray a 9 x 13-inch baking dish
with nonstick cooking spray.

Prepare and bake the cake according to the package directions for a 9 x 13-inch cake. Place the cake on a wire rack
and let cool completely.

Poke holes evenly over the cake using the tines of a fork.

Spoon the blueberry jam into a small microwave-safe glass
bowl. Microwave on High (100%) power for 20 seconds or
until melted. Spoon small dollops of jam, about ½ teaspoon each, over the top of the cake. Use the tip of a table
knife to gently spread the jam. (Spread the jam evenly, but
it will not fully cover the cake.)

Place the 1 cup water in a 4-cup microwave-safe glass bowl.
Microwave on High (100%) power for 2 to 3 minutes, or until
the water comes to a boil. Stir the gelatin into the water
until it has dissolved. Stir in the ½ cup cold water.

Slowly pour the raspberry gelatin mixture evenly over the
cake, filling the holes. Cover and refrigerate the cake for 1
hour.

Frost the cake with the whipped topping. Garnish the cake
with sliced strawberries, raspberries, and blueberries.

Boozy Poke Cakes

Pink Champagne Poke Cake

Pink Champagne Poke Cake personifies simple yet elegant ease. You can make any gathering into a special celebration with this recipe. Sprinkle the cake with edible pink glitter just before serving to add extra sparkle and bling to the table. This is fun served with pink Champagne, too!

Nonstick cooking spray

1 (15.25- to 18-ounce) box
  white cake mix

1 cup pink Champagne

¼ cup water

4 large eggs

⅓ cup vegetable or canola
  oil

Few drops red food coloring
  (optional)

¼ cup heavy cream

1 cup vanilla chips

Pink Champagne Frosting
  (page 149)

Preheat the oven to 350°F. Spray a 9 x 13-inch baking dish with nonstick cooking spray.

In a large bowl using a handheld mixer on low speed, beat together the cake mix, pink Champagne, water, eggs, and oil. Scrape down the sides of the bowl and beat on medium speed for 2 minutes. If a pink color is desired, add a few drops of red food coloring and blend thoroughly. Pour the batter into the prepared baking dish.

Bake for 28 to 32 minutes, or until a wooden pick inserted into the center of the cake comes out clean. Place the cake on a wire rack to cool for 10 minutes.

Poke holes evenly over the baked cake using a drinking straw.

In a 2-cup microwave-safe glass cup, stir together the cream and the vanilla chips. Microwave on Medium (50%) power in 30-second intervals, stirring after each, until melted and smooth. Pour the creamy sauce evenly over the top of the cake, filling the holes. Let cool completely.

Frost the cake with the Pink Champagne Frosting.

(continued)

Pink Champagne Poke Cake (continued)

VARIATION:

If you prefer, substitute lemon-lime-flavored soda or ginger ale for the Champagne.

Piña Colada Poke Cake

Do you like piña coladas (and getting caught in the rain)? We may be revealing our choice in music, but we definitely wouldn't pass up an opportunity to order that drink or to bake this delicious Piña Colada Poke Cake. If you like creamy coconut cocktails laced with rum, then this is the cake for you.

Nonstick cooking spray

1 (15.25- to 18-ounce) box yellow cake mix

Eggs and oil as directed on the cake mix box

1 (8-ounce) can crushed pineapple in juice, drained, juice reserved

1 (3.4-ounce) box coconut cream instant pudding mix

1¼ cups whole milk

½ cup cream of coconut

3 tablespoons dark rum

1 (8-ounce) tub frozen whipped topping, thawed

Toasted coconut, shredded or flaked (optional)

Preheat the oven to 350°F. Spray a 9 x 13-inch baking dish with nonstick cooking spray.

Prepare the cake according to the package directions for a 9 x 13-inch cake, substituting the reserved pineapple juice for the water called for on the cake mix box. (Add water, if needed, to equal the amount listed on the box.) Set the crushed pineapple aside. Bake as directed for a 9 x 13-inch cake.

Place the cake on a wire rack to cool for 10 minutes.

Poke holes evenly over the baked cake with the handle of a wooden spoon.

In a medium bowl, whisk together the pudding mix, milk, cream of coconut, and rum until the pudding is blended. Stir in the reserved crushed pineapple. Immediately pour the pudding mixture over the cake. Use the tip of a table knife to spread the pudding evenly, filling the holes. Cover and refrigerate the cake for 1 hour.

Frost the cake with the whipped topping. Cover and refrigerate the cake for at least 1 hour or up to overnight before serving.

Just before serving, garnish with toasted coconut, if desired.

VARIATION

If you prefer to omit the rum, increase the milk by 3 tablespoons. Whisk together the pudding mix, milk, and cream of coconut and proceed as the recipe directs.

 ✲ Cream of coconut is a thick, sweet mixture sold for use in cocktails. You will find it stocked with the cocktails and liquor in most grocery stores. Do not confuse it with coconut milk, which is often used in Asian food.

✲ Toasted coconut has a more intense flavor. To toast coconut, preheat the oven to 350°F. Spread the coconut evenly over a rimmed baking sheet. Bake, stirring occasionally, for 7 to 8 minutes, or until light golden brown. Let cool completely before sprinkling on the cake.

✲ If desired, substitute stiffly beaten sweetened whipped cream for the whipped topping. In a medium bowl, beat 1½ cups heavy cream with a handheld mixer on low speed until frothy. Increase the speed to medium-high. Gradually beat in 3 tablespoons confectioners' sugar; beat until the cream holds stiff peaks.

Bourbon Pecan Poke Cake

Imagine you are in the heartland of Kentucky, where there is only one drink to be reckoned with, and that drink is bourbon. Now, in that same heartland rich with bourbon distilleries, there is a wedding of bourbon and toasty pecans, and you were invited. Celebrate the joy of this match made in heaven with Bourbon Pecan Poke Cake.

Nonstick cooking spray

1 (15.25- to 18-ounce) box
yellow cake mix

1 cup sour cream

⅓ cup vegetable or canola
oil

¼ cup water

4 large eggs

⅓ cup plus 1 tablespoon
bourbon

Bourbon Pecan Caramel
Frosting (page 145)

TIP

For a deeper pecan flavor,
substitute a butter pecan cake
mix for the yellow cake mix.
Proceed with the recipe as
directed.

Preheat the oven to 350°F. Spray a 9 x 13-inch baking dish with nonstick cooking spray.

In a large bowl using a handheld mixer on low speed, beat together the cake mix, sour cream, oil, water, eggs, and 1 tablespoon of the bourbon. Scrape down the sides of the bowl and beat on medium speed for 2 minutes. Pour the batter into the prepared pan.

Bake for 28 to 30 minutes, or until a wooden pick inserted into the center of the cake comes out clean. Place the cake on a wire rack and let cool completely.

Poke holes evenly over the baked cake using the tines of a fork. Drizzle the remaining ⅓ cup bourbon in a thin stream over the poked holes and allow to seep into cake.

Frost the cake with the Bourbon Pecan Caramel Frosting. Serve warm or at room temperature.

Golden Rum-Glazed Layer Poke Cake

Roxanne grew up in Independence, Missouri, and has fond memories of a special rum cake that was served at V's Italian Restaurant. Pep club banquets, rehearsal dinners, and even Roxanne's mom Colleen's retirement dinner were celebrated at V's. Each and every meal at V's is served with V's famous rum cake. Hours and hours of testing and sampling went into this recipe to try to replicate Roxanne's memory as closely as possible. We think we nailed it and hope you will give it a try.

Nonstick cooking spray

1 (15.25- to 18-ounce) box yellow cake mix

1 (3.4-ounce) box vanilla instant pudding mix

4 large eggs

½ cup water

½ cup canola or vegetable oil

½ cup dark rum

¼ cup packed dark brown sugar

2 teaspoons ground cinnamon

RUM GLAZE:

6 tablespoons (3/4 stick) unsalted butter

2 tablespoons water

¾ cup sugar

6 tablespoons dark rum

Marshmallow Frosting (page 148)

Preheat the oven to 350°F. Spray two 9-inch round cake pans with nonstick cooking spray. Line the bottoms of the pans with parchment paper cut to fit and spray the parchment as well.

In a large bowl using a handheld mixer on low speed, beat together the cake mix, pudding mix, eggs, water, oil, and rum. Scrape down the sides of the bowl well and beat for 2 minutes on medium speed.

In a small bowl, stir together the brown sugar and cinnamon. Pour one-quarter of the batter into each prepared pan. Sprinkle the cinnamon–brown sugar mixture evenly between the two pans. Top each pan with one-quarter more batter.

Bake for 24 to 27 minutes, or until a wooden pick inserted into the center of the cakes comes out clean. Place the cakes on a wire rack to cool for 5 minutes.

Poke holes evenly over each baked cake layer using the tines of a fork.

MAKE THE RUM GLAZE: While the cake is baking, in a medium saucepan, melt the butter over medium heat. Stir in the water and sugar; bring the mixture to a boil, stirring frequently, and boil for 4 to 5 minutes. Remove from the heat and carefully add the rum. Stir to combine well.

(continued)

Be very careful when adding the rum to the hot glaze mixture. It may bubble and splatter, so add the rum very slowly.

Drizzle half the rum glaze over each cake layer, being sure to drizzle it into the poked holes. Let cool for 10 minutes.

Place a large plate over one of the layers and invert to remove the cake from the pan. Remove the parchment paper. Use another large plate to invert the layer back so the side with the rum glaze remains on top. Repeat the process with the second layer. Let the layers cool completely before frosting.

Place half of the Marshmellow Frosting on the top side of one layer. Top with the second layer, glazed-side up, and frost the top with the remaining frosting. (The sides will not be frosted.)

Limoncello Cake

Jasper's Italian restaurant is famous for being one of the best places in Kansas City to dine and enjoy authentic Italian food in the city. Almost as famous as the restaurant is the limoncello cake that Jasper Mirabile Jr. bakes. We were honored and thrilled when Jasper agreed to let us share his famous recipe with you. Limoncello Cake is truly a poke cake that deserves a place in the poke cake hall of fame. Grazie, Jasper!

Nonstick baking spray with
  flour
1 (15.25- to 18-ounce) box
  yellow cake mix
1 (3.4-ounce) box vanilla
  instant pudding mix
¾ cup limoncello
½ cup canola or vegetable
  oil
¼ cup water
4 large eggs
1 large egg yolk
Grated zest of 1 large lemon

GLAZE:
¾ cup packed dark brown
  sugar
¾ cup (1½ sticks) unsalted
  butter
¼ cup limoncello
Grated zest of 1 large lemon
3 tablespoons fresh lemon
  juice

Preheat the oven to 350°F. Spray a 12-cup Bundt pan with nonstick baking spray with flour.

In a large bowl using a handheld mixer on low speed, beat together the cake mix, pudding mix, limoncello, oil, water, eggs, egg yolk, and lemon zest. Scrape down the sides of the bowl well and beat for 2 minutes on medium speed. Pour the batter into the prepared pan.

Bake for 55 to 60 minutes, or until a wooden pick inserted into the center of the cake comes out clean. Place the cake on a wire rack to cool for 5 to 10 minutes.

MAKE THE GLAZE: While cake is baking, in a small saucepan, combine the brown sugar, butter, limoncello, lemon zest, and lemon juice. Bring to a boil over medium heat, stirring continuously. Cook, stirring continuously, for 4 to 5 minutes, or until the mixture has a creamy consistency.

Line a rimmed baking sheet with aluminum foil (to make cleanup easy). Place a wire rack on the foil-lined baking sheet. Invert the cake onto the wire rack and remove the pan.

TIP

Placing the cake on a wire rack and letting the excess glaze drip off ensures that the bottom of the cake does not become soggy from sitting in the glaze. To easily move the cake from the wire rack to the cake plate, use two long pancake turners to carefully lift the cake.

Poke holes evenly over the top of the baked cake using a skewer. Spoon the glaze slowly over the cake and into poked holes. The glaze will run down the sides. Let the cake cool for at least 1 hour before serving.

Carefully move the cake to a cake plate and serve.

Tequila Sunrise Poke Cake

Sunrise paints a graduated array of colors as the deep orange and red fade into yellow. That beautiful view is what gave this historic drink its name. While the drink is as old as the Prohibition era, it became popular in the 1970s when a bar in Sausalito, near San Francisco, reinvented it and traveling musicians from famous rock bands tasted it and helped seal its place in pop culture. The current drink is made of orange juice, grenadine, and tequila—and this cake captures those wonderful flavors and the striking colors:

Nonstick cooking spray

1 (15.25- to 18-ounce) box yellow cake mix

Eggs, oil, and water as directed on the cake mix

1 cup water

1 (3-ounce) box orange gelatin

¼ cup tequila

3 tablespoons grenadine syrup

1 (8-ounce) tub frozen whipped topping, thawed

Preheat the oven to 350°F. Spray a 9 x 13-inch baking dish with nonstick cooking spray.

Prepare and bake the cake according to the package directions for a 9 x 13-inch cake. Place cake on a wire rack to cool for 10 minutes.

Poke holes evenly over the baked cake using the tines of a fork.

Place the water in a 4-cup microwave-safe glass bowl. Microwave on High (100%) power for 2 to 3 minutes, or until the water comes to a boil. Stir the gelatin into the water until it is dissolved. Stir in the tequila. Pour the gelatin mixture evenly over the cake.

Slowly and evenly drizzle the cake with the grenadine, making a striped design across the cake. Cover and refrigerate the cake for 1 hour.

Frost the cake with the whipped topping. Cover and refrigerate the cake for at least 1 hour or up to overnight before serving.

(continued)

VARIATIONS

If you prefer to omit the tequila, prepare the gelatin as directed. Stir in ¼ cup cold water and proceed as the recipe directs.

If desired, instead of using all water to prepare the cake mix, substitute ¼ cup tequila and ½ cup orange juice for part of the water. Add water, as needed, to equal the required amount of liquid specified on the cake mix box. Proceed as the recipe directs.

✳ Grenadine is a sweet, red syrup that is often used to flavor cocktails. While it is not a liquor, you will often find it in the grocery store shelved with mixers and supplies for cocktails.

If desired, omit the whipped topping and substitute Orange Liqueur Buttercream Frosting (page 144).

Margarita Poke Cake

It is Friday night and that is the perfect time to grab a margarita with your friends. What fun! But why wait for a night out? This cake has all the flavors and the fun of that famous drink.

Nonstick cooking spray

1 (15.25- to 18-ounce) box white cake mix

Eggs, oil, and water as directed on the cake mix box

⅓ cup sugar

⅓ cup fresh lime juice

¼ cup tequila

1 or 2 drops green food coloring

1 or 2 drops yellow food coloring

Orange Liqueur Buttercream Frosting (page 144)

Preheat the oven to 350°F. Spray a 9 x 13-inch baking dish with nonstick cooking spray.

Prepare and bake the cake according to the package directions for a 9 x 13-inch cake. Place the cake on a wire rack to cool for 10 minutes.

Poke holes evenly over the baked cake using the tines of a fork.

In a small saucepan, combine the sugar and lime juice. Heat over medium heat, stirring frequently, until boiling. Reduce the heat to low and cook, uncovered, for 3 minutes, stirring frequently. Remove from the heat and stir in the tequila. Tint lightly with the food coloring to a lime color. Slowly and evenly drizzle the hot syrup over the cake. Let stand for 30 minutes.

Frost the cake with the Orange Liqueur Buttercream Frosting.

VARIATION

Do you prefer to make the cake without liquor? Make the sugar and lime syrup as directed, but omit the tequila. Proceed as the recipe directs. Frost with Orange Buttercream Frosting (page 144).

Mint Julep Poke Cake

Horse races, big hats, roses, and mint juleps to drink. Doesn't it sound fun? While we have never attended the race, we both love mint juleps. Now we have captured the great flavor of that drink in this luscious Mint Julep Poke Cake. It is a winner!

Mint Julep Syrup (recipe
  below)
Nonstick cooking spray
1 (15.25- to 18-ounce) box
  white cake mix
3 large eggs
1¼ cups buttermilk
6 tablespoons (3/4 stick)
  unsalted butter, melted

MINT JULEP SYRUP:
¼ cup sugar
¼ cup water
¼ cup fresh mint leaves
¼ cup bourbon
¼ cup confectioners' sugar,
  sifted
2 tablespoons unsalted
  butter, melted

Vanilla Buttercream Frosting
  (page 144)

Preheat the oven to 350°F. Spray a 9 x 13-inch baking dish with nonstick cooking spray.

In a large bowl using a handheld mixer on low speed, blend together the cake mix, eggs, buttermilk, and melted butter. Scrape down the sides of the bowl well and beat for 2 minutes on medium speed. Pour the batter into the prepared baking dish.

Bake for 30 to 35 minutes, or until a wooden pick inserted into the center of the cake comes out clean. Place the cake on a wire rack to cool for 10 minutes.

MAKE THE MINT JULEP SYRUP: While the cake is baking, in a small saucepan, combine the sugar and the water. Heat over medium heat, stirring frequently, until boiling. Stir to dissolve the sugar. Remove from the heat. Stir in the mint leaves. Use a muddler or the back of a spoon to bruise the leaves; set aside to steep for about 30 minutes.

Pour the syrup through a strainer into a small bowl to remove the mint leaves; discard the mint leaves. Stir in the bourbon, confectioners' sugar, and melted butter; stir until smooth.

Poke holes evenly over the baked cake using the tines of a fork. Drizzle the Mint Julep Syrup over the cake. Let stand for 30 minutes.

Frost the cake with the Vanilla Buttercream Frosting.

(continued)

VARIATION:

If you prefer, omit the bourbon. Make the mint syrup as directed, using 6 tablespoons sugar and 6 tablespoons water. Proceed as the recipe directs.

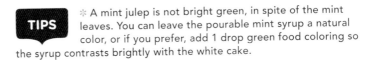 ✳ A mint julep is not bright green, in spite of the mint leaves. You can leave the pourable mint syrup a natural color, or if you prefer, add 1 drop green food coloring so the syrup contrasts brightly with the white cake.

✳ Do you especially like mint? Frost the cake with Mint Buttercream Frosting (page 144.)

Orange Liqueur Poke Cake

A luxurious sip of Grand Marnier, that special blend of cognac and oranges, may be a delicious escape on a busy day. You might think of using this wonderful liqueur in a signature cocktail or enjoy an elegant drink after dinner. For the scrumptious Orange Liqueur Poke Cake, drizzle that famous orange liqueur over a Bundt cake.

Nonstick baking spray with flour

1 (15.25- to 18-ounce) box yellow cake mix

1 (3.4-ounce) box vanilla instant pudding mix

1 (11-ounce) can mandarin oranges in light syrup, drained, syrup reserved

4 large eggs

½ cup canola or vegetable oil

¼ cup Grand Marnier or other orange liqueur

GRAND MARNIER GLAZE:

1 cup confectioners' sugar

1 to 2 tablespoons Grand Marnier or other orange liqueur

Preheat the oven to 350°F. Spray a 12-cup Bundt pan with nonstick baking spray with flour.

In a large bowl using a handheld mixer on low speed, beat together the cake mix, pudding mix, mandarin oranges, eggs, oil, and ¼ cup of the reserved mandarin orange syrup. Scrape down the sides of the bowl well and beat for 2 minutes on medium speed. Pour the batter into the prepared pan. (Discard any remaining orange syrup.)

Bake for 37 to 42 minutes, or until a wooden pick inserted into the center of the cake comes out clean. Place the cake on a wire rack and cool for 5 minutes.

Using a skewer, poke holes evenly over the surface of the cake before removing it from the pan. Drizzle the Grand Marnier over the cake, allowing it to soak into the cake. Let cool for 15 minutes.

Line a rimmed baking sheet with aluminum foil (to make cleanup easy). Place a wire rack on the foil-lined baking sheet. Invert the cake onto the wire rack and remove the pan. Poke holes evenly over the top of the cake using a skewer.

MAKE THE GRAND MARNIER GLAZE: In a small bowl, stir together the confectioners' sugar and 1 tablespoon of the Grand Marnier. If a thinner glaze is desired, blend in the remaining 1 tablespoon Grand Marnier.

Drizzle the glaze over the cake. Let cool completely.

Carefully move the cake to a cake plate and serve.

Honey Whiskey Poke Cake

Are bourbon and whiskey the same thing? Well, not exactly. Bourbon must be made in the United States with at least 51 percent corn. Tennessee whiskey must be distilled in Tennessee. Think about Champagne—it's only Champagne if it is made in France. We recommend that an American whiskey or bourbon be used in this recipe. Start a new tradition; in lieu of a "nightcap," enjoy a slice of this honey-infused whiskey cake, and you are guaranteed sweet dreams.

Nonstick baking spray with flour
1 (15.25- to 18-ounce) box yellow cake mix
1 (3.4-ounce) box vanilla instant pudding mix
½ cup whole milk
⅓ cup whiskey or bourbon
4 large eggs
3 tablespoons honey
1 teaspoon pure vanilla extract
1 cup chopped pecans, toasted

GLAZE:
½ cup (1 stick) unsalted butter
½ cup sugar
2 tablespoons water
½ cup whiskey or bourbon
¼ cup honey

Preheat the oven to 350°F. Spray a 12-cup Bundt pan with nonstick baking spray with flour.

In a large bowl using a handheld mixer on low speed, beat together the cake mix, pudding mix, milk, whiskey, eggs, honey, and vanilla extract. Scrape down the sides of the bowl well and beat for 2 minutes on medium speed. Fold in the pecans with a spatula. Pour the batter into the prepared baking pan.

Bake for 35 to 40 minutes, or until a wooden pick inserted into the center of the cake comes out clean. Place the cake on a wire rack while preparing the glaze.

MAKE THE GLAZE: In a medium saucepan, bring the butter, sugar, and water to a boil over medium-high heat. Reduce the heat to maintain a simmer and cook for several minutes, until the sugar has dissolved. Remove from the heat and add the whiskey. Return to the heat and cook for about a minute. Remove from the heat and add the honey. Stir until blended.

Using a skewer, poke holes evenly over the surface of the cake before removing it from the pan.

Carefully spoon about half the glaze over the cake.

TIP

If desired, serve with a dollop of whipped cream or a small scoop of vanilla ice cream.

Line a rimmed baking sheet with aluminum foil (to make cleanup easy). Place a wire rack on the foil-lined baking sheet. Invert the cake onto the wire rack and remove the pan. Poke holes evenly over the top of the baked cake using a skewer. Spoon the remaining glaze over the cake. Let cool completely.

Carefully move the cake to a cake plate and serve.

Coffee Liqueur and Cream Poke Cake

Kahlúa, the coffee liqueur, and cream is kind of like an adult café au lait. It was a popular cocktail long before every corner had a coffee shop that served café au laits. The timeless cocktail is smooth, creamy, and oh, so good! This Coffee Liqueur and Cream Poke Cake features that same superb flavor—a chocolate cake poked with a creamy Kahlúa filling, then topped with whipped cream. It is a classic!

Nonstick cooking spray

1 (15.25- to 18-ounce) box devil's food cake mix

Eggs and oil as directed on the cake mix box

Whole milk, in place of the water called for on the cake mix box

1 (3.4-ounce) box vanilla instant pudding mix

1 cup heavy cream

½ cup whole milk

¼ cup Kahlúa

KAHLÚA WHIPPED CREAM TOPPING:

1½ cups heavy cream

3 tablespoons confectioners' sugar

1 tablespoon Kahlúa

Preheat the oven to 350°F. Spray a 9 x 13-inch baking dish with nonstick cooking spray.

Prepare and bake the cake according to the package directions, substituting milk for the water called for on the box. Bake according to the package directions for a 9 x 13-inch cake. Place the cake on a wire rack and let cool completely.

Poke holes evenly over the cake using a drinking straw.

In a medium bowl, whisk together the pudding mix with the cream and the milk until the pudding is blended. Stir in the Kahlúa. Pour the pudding over the top of the cake, spreading it evenly and filling in the poked holes. Cover and refrigerate the cake for 1 hour.

MAKE THE KAHLÚA WHIPPED CREAM TOPPING: In a medium bowl using a handheld mixer, beat the cream on low speed until frothy. Increase the speed to medium-high. Gradually beat in the confectioners' sugar, beating continuously until the cream holds stiff peaks. Beat in the Kahlúa.

Frost the cake with the Kahlúa Whipped Cream Topping. Refrigerate until ready to serve.

VARIATION:

If you prefer, omit the Kahlúa. Substitute strong, brewed, lightly sweetened coffee, cooled to room temperature, for the Kahlúa.

Bundt Poke Cakes

Peaches 'n' Cream Bundt Poke Cake

Is it any wonder that nectar was professed to be the drink of the Greek and Roman gods? I think not, for with one sip, you will enter another world. The use of peach nectar throughout this recipe assures a sweet, peach-filled taste that is sure to please. When fresh peaches are in season, garnish the whipped cream with a slice or two.

Nonstick baking spray with flour

1 (15.25- to 18-ounce) box vanilla cake mix

1 (3-ounce) box peach gelatin

1 cup peach nectar

½ cup canola or vegetable oil

4 large eggs

1 (14.5-ounce) can no-sugar-added sliced peaches, drained

GLAZE:

¾ cup confectioners' sugar

3 tablespoons peach nectar

Whipped cream or frozen whipped topping, thawed

TIP

⁎ If fresh peaches are in season, substitute 1¼ cups diced peeled peaches for the canned peaches.

Preheat the oven to 350°F. Spray a 12-cup Bundt pan with nonstick baking spray with flour.

In a large bowl using a handheld mixer on low speed, beat together the cake mix, gelatin, nectar, oil, and eggs. Scrape down the sides of the bowl well and beat for 2 minutes on medium speed. Drain the peaches on paper towels and pat dry. Slice each peach slice into small pieces. Gently fold the sliced peaches into the batter using a spatula. Pour the batter into the prepared baking pan.

Bake for 40 to 45 minutes, or until a wooden pick inserted into the center of the cake comes out clean. Place the cake on a wire rack to cool for 10 minutes.

MAKE THE GLAZE: In a small bowl, whisk together the confectioners' sugar and nectar.

Using a skewer, poke holes evenly over the surface of the cake. Using a large spoon, drizzle half the glaze over the cake in the pan. Let cool for 10 minutes more.

Line a rimmed baking sheet with aluminum foil (to make cleanup easy). Place a wire rack on the foil-lined baking sheet. Invert the cake onto the wire rack and remove the pan. Poke holes evenly over the top of the baked cake using a skewer. Drizzle the remaining glaze into the holes.

Carefully move the cake to a cake plate and serve. Dollop each slice with whipped cream or whipped topping.

Triple Citrus Bundt Poke Cake

You really wouldn't pick one of your children over the other, would you? Of course not! You love your children equally. The same is true with limes, oranges, and lemons. We love them all equally, and now we don't have to choose to enjoy the tangy flavor of each. We've created citrus bliss!

Nonstick baking spray with flour

1 (15.25- to 18-ounce) box yellow cake mix

1 (6-ounce) container key lime or lime yogurt

½ cup canola or vegetable oil

4 large eggs

SYRUP TOPPING:

⅓ cup fresh lemon juice

3 tablespoons orange juice

½ cup superfine sugar

ICING:

1 cup confectioners' sugar, sifted

2 to 3 tablespoons fresh lemon juice

TIP

This cake is delicious served with a dollop of whipped cream flavored with a bit of lime, orange, or lemon zest.

Preheat the oven to 350°F. Spray a 12-cup Bundt pan with nonstick baking spray with flour.

In a large bowl using a handheld mixer on low speed, beat together the cake mix, yogurt, oil, and eggs. Scrape down the sides of the bowl well and beat for 2 minutes on medium speed. Pour the batter into the prepared baking pan.

Bake for 35 to 40 minutes, or until a wooden pick inserted into the center of the cake comes out clean. Place the cake on a wire rack to cool for 10 minutes.

Line a rimmed baking sheet with aluminum foil (to make cleanup easy). Place a wire rack on the foil-lined baking sheet. Invert the cake onto the wire rack and remove the pan. Poke holes evenly over the top of the baked cake using a skewer.

MAKE THE SYRUP TOPPING: In a small saucepan, combine the lemon juice, orange juice, and superfine sugar. Bring to a boil over medium-high heat. Boil for 1 minute. Using a large spoon, carefully pour the syrup over the top of the cake and into the holes. Let cool completely.

MAKE THE ICING: In a small bowl, whisk together the confectioners' sugar and lemon juice until smooth. Drizzle over the cooled cake.

Carefully move the cake to a cake plate and serve.

Pineapple Bundt Poke Cake

When would we serve this cake? Oh, let us count the many ways—for coffee with friends, after brunch, as a delightful treat after lunch, for an afternoon snack at the office, as the sweet after an elegant dinner, as the perfect cake to take to a potluck—and every other time you need a great dessert.

Nonstick baking spray with flour

1 (15.25- to 18-ounce) vanilla or French vanilla cake mix

1 (3.4-ounce) box vanilla instant pudding

4 large eggs

½ cup canola or vegetable oil

1 (20-ounce) can crushed pineapple in juice, well drained, juice reserved

1 tablespoon unsalted butter, melted

1¼ cups confectioners' sugar

TIP

To be sure the pineapple is well drained, pour the fruit into a strainer set over a small bowl and press lightly on the fruit with the back of a spoon.

Preheat the oven to 350°F. Spray a 12-cup Bundt pan with nonstick baking spray with flour.

In a large bowl using a handheld mixer on low speed, beat together the cake mix, pudding mix, eggs, oil, and ¾ cup of the reserved pineapple juice (reserve the remaining juice for the syrup and glaze). Scrape down the sides of the bowl well and beat for 2 minutes on medium speed. Stir the drained crushed pineapple into the batter. Pour the batter into the prepared baking pan.

Bake for 45 to 50 minutes, or until a wooden pick inserted into the center of the cake comes out clean. Place the cake on a wire rack to cool for 5 minutes.

In a small bowl, stir together the melted butter, ½ cup of the confectioners' sugar, and 2 tablespoons of the reserved pineapple juice until smooth.

Using a skewer, poke holes evenly over the surface of the cake. Drizzle the melted butter mixture over the cake, allowing it to soak into the cake. Let cool for 30 minutes.

Line a rimmed baking sheet with aluminum foil (to make cleanup easy). Place a wire rack on the foil-lined baking sheet. Invert the cake onto the wire rack and remove the pan. Poke holes evenly over the top of the baked cake using a skewer.

In a small bowl, stir together the remaining ¾ cup confectioners' sugar and 2 tablespoons of the reserved pineapple juice until smooth. Drizzle over the top of the cake. Carefully move the cake to a cake plate and serve.

Pumpkin Bundt Poke Cake

People always ask us which recipe in a cookbook is our favorite, and that is a tough question. Each recipe is special, and we like them all (or they wouldn't be in the book). But there is something about the combination of pumpkin, maple syrup, and cream that makes this cake especially good. In fact, it just might be Kathy's favorite.

Nonstick baking spray with flour

1 (15.25- to 18-ounce) yellow cake mix

1 (15-ounce) can pure pumpkin puree

3 large eggs

⅓ cup canola or vegetable oil

1 teaspoon pumpkin pie spice

¾ cup maple syrup or maple-flavored pancake syrup

6 tablespoons heavy cream

1½ tablespoons unsalted butter

Confectioners' sugar, for dusting

Preheat the oven to 350°F. Spray a 12-cup Bundt pan with nonstick baking spray with flour.

In a large bowl using a handheld mixer on low speed, beat together the cake mix, pumpkin puree, eggs, oil, and pumpkin pie spice. Scrape down the sides of the bowl well and beat for 2 minutes on medium speed. Pour the batter into the prepared baking pan.

Bake for 45 to 50 minutes, or until a wooden pick inserted into the center of the cake comes out clean. Place the cake on a wire rack to cool for 5 minutes.

In a small saucepan, combine the maple syrup, cream, and butter. Cook over medium-low heat, stirring frequently, until the butter has melted and the mixture is smooth and hot, about 5 minutes.

Using a skewer, poke holes evenly over the surface of the cake. Slowly drizzle about half the maple syrup mixture over the cake. Reserve the remaining syrup in the saucepan. Let the cake cool for 30 minutes.

Line a rimmed baking sheet with aluminum foil (to make cleanup easy). Place a wire rack on the foil-lined baking sheet. Invert the cake onto the wire rack and remove the pan. Poke holes evenly over the top of the baked cake using a skewer. Heat the remaining syrup in the saucepan over low heat, stirring continuously, just until the syrup is warm. Slowly pour the syrup over the cake. Let cool completely.

Carefully move the cake to a cake plate. Dust with the confectioners' sugar just before serving.

Lemon Blueberry Bundt Poke Cake

Lemon Blueberry Bundt Poke Cake is one of the best ways to enjoy vibrant lemon flavor. Serve this delicious cake on warm summer nights or when you have a picnic planned with family and friends. Whenever you serve it, the flavors of the lemon and sweet blueberries come together in perfect harmony.

Nonstick baking spray with flour
1 (15.25- to 18-ounce) box lemon cake mix
1 (3-ounce) box lemon gelatin
2/3 cup water
2/3 cup vegetable or canola oil
4 large eggs
1¼ cups fresh blueberries

CITRUS POKE GLAZE
Grated zest of 2 small or 1 large lemon
Juice of 2 small or 1 large lemon (about ¼ cup)
1 cup confectioners' sugar

Preheat the oven to 350°F. Spray a 12-cup Bundt pan with nonstick baking spray with flour.

Remove 2 tablespoons of the cake mix and place in a 3-cup bowl; set aside.

In a large bowl using a handheld mixer on low speed, beat together the remaining cake mix, gelatin, water, oil and eggs. Scrape down the sides of the bowl well and beat for 2 minutes on medium speed.

Pat the blueberries dry with paper towels. Toss the blueberries with the reserved cake mix and then fold into the batter. Pour the batter into the prepared baking pan, smoothing the top evenly with a spatula.

Bake for 35 to 45 minutes or until a wooden pick inserted into the center of the cake comes out clean. Place the cake on a wire rack.

Using a skewer, poke holes evenly over the surface of the cake.

MAKE THE CITRUS POKE GLAZE: In a medium bowl, whisk together the lemon zest, lemon juice, and confectioners' sugar until smooth. Using a large spoon, drizzle about half the glaze over the warm cake. Let cool for 10 minutes.

Line a rimmed baking sheet with aluminum foil (to make cleanup easy). Place a wire rack on the foil-lined baking sheet. Invert the cake onto the rack and remove the pan. Let cool completely.

TIPS

✳ Substitute frozen blueberries for fresh, if needed. Do not thaw the frozen blueberries.

✳ When grating the lemon zest, grate just the outer yellow portion. That is where the delicious flavor is found. The white pith underneath is bitter.

✳ Serve the cake with a dollop of sweetened, whipped cream.

Poke holes evenly over the top of the baked cake using a skewer. Using a large spoon, drizzle the remaining glaze evenly over the top of the cake, allowing the glaze to seep into the holes.

Carefully move the cake to a cake plate. Serve the cake warm or at room temperature.

Caramel Apple Bundt Poke Cake

Classic flavors come together to make this Caramel Apple Bundt Poke Cake. Kathy made this cake to take to a family reunion, and it was a hit. It stayed moist, and even though there were several desserts, the plate this cake was on was the first to turn up empty. It's a winner!

Nonstick baking spray with flour

1 (15.25- to 18-ounce) spice cake mix

4 large eggs

1 cup sour cream

½ cup canola or vegetable oil

2 medium crisp apples, peeled, cored, and chopped

½ cup chopped pecans or walnuts, toasted (optional)

⅔ cup caramel ice cream topping

BROWN SUGAR GLAZE:

3 tablespoons unsalted butter

¼ cup packed brown sugar

2 tablespoons whole milk

1 cup confectioners' sugar, sifted

½ teaspoon pure vanilla extract

Preheat the oven to 350°F. Spray a 12-cup Bundt pan with nonstick baking spray with flour.

In a large bowl using a handheld mixer on low speed, beat together the cake mix, eggs, sour cream, and oil. Scrape down the sides of the bowl well and beat for 2 minutes on medium speed. Stir in the chopped apples and the pecans (if using). Pour the batter into the prepared baking pan.

Bake for 45 to 50 minutes, or until wooden pick inserted into the center of the cake comes out clean. Place the cake on a wire rack to cool for 5 minutes.

Pour ⅓ cup of the caramel topping into a microwave-safe glass bowl. Microwave on High (100%) power for 20 seconds, or until warm.

Using a skewer, poke holes evenly over the surface of the cake. Drizzle the warm caramel evenly over the cake and allow it to soak in. Let cool for 15 minutes.

Line a rimmed baking sheet with aluminum foil (to make cleanup easy). Place a wire rack on the foil-lined baking sheet. Invert the cake onto the wire rack and remove the pan. Let cool completely.

Poke holes evenly over the top of the baked cake using a skewer. Pour the remaining ⅓ cup caramel topping into a microwave-safe glass bowl. Microwave on High (100%) power for 20 seconds, or until warm. Drizzle the caramel topping over the top of the cake, allowing it to soak into the cake. Let stand for 30 minutes. *(continued)*

What kind of apples to use? Crisp apples are especially good for baking, and Granny Smith are perfect for this cake.

MAKE THE BROWN SUGAR GLAZE: In a small saucepan, melt the butter and brown sugar over medium heat, stirring frequently, until the mixture comes to a boil. Cook, stirring continuously, for 1 minute. Remove from the heat. Stir in the milk and confectioners' sugar. Add the vanilla and stir until the mixture is smooth. Drizzle the glaze over the top of the cake.

Carefully move the cake to a cake plate and serve.

Frostings

Frosting, sweet and creamy or light and fluffy, is the crowning glory on many cakes. In this chapter, we offer a collection of several of our favorite frostings and have topped many of the poke cakes with them. You can always exchange our recommended frosting for a flavor of your own choice, or choose to top the poke cake with whipped cream, thawed frozen whipped topping, or another prepared frosting.

Do you prefer softer or firmer frostings? Both are great, but if you like softer frostings, beat in additional milk, cream, or half-and-half, 1 to 2 tablespoons or as needed, to make the frosting the ideal spreading consistency and create a frosting just the way you like it. Similarly, add 1 to 2 tablespoons confectioners' sugar if you prefer a thicker frosting.

MAKES ABOUT 3 CUPS

Cream Cheese Frosting

1 (8-ounce) package cream cheese, softened
½ cup (1 stick) unsalted butter, softened
4 cups confectioners' sugar
1 teaspoon pure vanilla extract

In a large bowl using a handheld mixer on medium speed, beat the cream cheese until smooth. Add the remaining ingredients and beat until smooth and creamy. The frosting should be a nice spreading consistency.

VARIATIONS

ALMOND CREAM CHEESE FROSTING: Omit the vanilla extract. Add ½ teaspoon pure almond extract. If an intense almond flavor is desired, increase the almond extract to 1 teaspoon.

LIME CREAM CHEESE FROSTING: Omit the vanilla extract and add 1 teaspoon grated lime zest and 1 to 2 teaspoons fresh lime juice.

Vanilla Buttercream Frosting

½ cup (1 stick) unsalted
  butter, softened
4 cups confectioners' sugar
4 to 6 tablespoons whole
  milk
1 teaspoon pure vanilla
  extract

In a large bowl using a handheld mixer on medium speed, beat the butter until creamy. Gradually beat in the sugar. Beat in 4 tablespoons of the milk and the vanilla until smooth and creamy. If necessary for a nice spreading consistency, add the remaining 1 to 2 tablespoons milk.

VARIATIONS

MINT BUTTERCREAM: Stir in ½ teaspoon peppermint extract and 3 or 4 drops green food coloring.

ORANGE BUTTERCREAM: Substitute orange juice for the milk.

ORANGE LIQUEUR BUTTERCREAM: Substitute 2 tablespoons Grand Marnier or other orange liqueur and 2 to 4 tablespoons orange juice for the milk.

Caramel Frosting

¾ cup packed dark brown
   sugar
6 tablespoons (3/4 stick)
   unsalted butter
¼ cup heavy cream
1½ cups confectioners'
   sugar
1 teaspoon pure vanilla
   extract

Do you prefer a thick layer of
luscious caramel frosting? If
so, double the recipe.

In a small saucepan, combine the brown sugar, butter and
cream. Heat over medium heat, stirring occasionally, until
the butter has melted. Bring the mixture to a boil and cook,
stirring continuously, for about 1 minute. Remove from the
heat. Add the confectioners' sugar and vanilla. Using a
handheld mixer, beat on low speed until combined. (Alternatively, if you do not want to use your mixer in the saucepan, transfer the butter mixture to a large bowl.) Increase
the speed to medium and beat until the mixture is slightly
thickened and a nice spreading consistency.

VARIATION

BOURBON PECAN CARAMEL: Omit the vanilla and add
1 tablespoon bourbon. Blend until smooth. Stir in ¾ cup
coarsely chopped toasted pecans.

Chocolate Frosting

½ cup (1 stick) unsalted butter, cut into ½-inch slices

⅔ cup unsweetened cocoa powder

3 cups confectioners' sugar

3 tablespoons whole milk

1 teaspoon pure vanilla extract

In a medium saucepan, melt the butter over low heat. Stir in the cocoa powder and remove the pan from the heat. Add the confectioners' sugar, milk, and vanilla and, using a handheld mixer, beat on medium-high speed until smooth and creamy. (Alternatively, if you do not want to use your mixer in the saucepan, transfer the butter mixture to a large bowl and proceed as directed.)

Easy Decorator's Frosting

½ cup (1 stick) unsalted
   butter or margarine,
   softened
½ cup vegetable shortening
4 cups confectioners' sugar
1 teaspoon pure vanilla
   extract
2 to 3 tablespoons whole
   milk

In a large bowl using a handheld mixer on medium speed, beat together the butter and shortening. Add the confectioners' sugar, vanilla, and 2 tablespoons of the milk. Continue to blend when the sugar is incorporated, increase the speed to medium-high and beat until the frosting is creamy and fluffy. If necessary for a nice spreading consistency, add the remaining 1 tablespoon milk.

 TIP If not using immediately, store in an airtight container in the refrigerator for up to 3 weeks.

Marshmallow Frosting

½ cup (1 stick) unsalted
   butter, softened
⅓ cup confectioners' sugar
1 (7½-ounce) jar
   marshmallow creme
1 tablespoon whole milk

In a large bowl using a handheld mixer, beat the butter on medium speed until creamy. Add the confectioners' sugar, marshmallow creme, and milk and beat on medium to medium-high speed until frosting is smooth, creamy, and a nice spreading consistency.

White Chocolate Frosting

1 (4-ounce) package white
   chocolate, chopped
1 (8-ounce) package cream
   cheese, softened
½ cup (1 stick) unsalted
   butter, softened
4 cups confectioners' sugar

Melt the white chocolate according to the package directions. Let cool until just warm.

In a large bowl using a handheld mixer on medium-high speed, beat the cream cheese and butter until creamy. Beat in the melted white chocolate and confectioners' sugar until smooth and creamy.

 TIP If you beat the melted white chocolate into the frosting while the white chocolate is still quite hot, the frosting will be very thin. Allow the white chocolate to cool until just warm.

Pink Champagne Frosting

½ cup (1 stick) unsalted
   butter, softened
6 to 7 cups confectioner's
   sugar
½ cup pink Champagne
1 tablespoon whole milk
Few drops red food coloring

In a large bowl using a handheld mixer, beat the butter on high speed until creamy. Add 6 cups of the confectioners' sugar, the Champagne, and the milk. Beat until smooth and creamy. If needed to get a nice spreading consistency, add the remaining 1 cup confectioners' sugar.

VARIATION

If you prefer to omit the Champagne, substitute lemon-lime-flavored soda or ginger ale.

Acknowledgments

Roxanne's family: I want to thank my husband, Bob Bateman, and my daughter, Grace. You are part of every book we write. You are my cake, my frosting, and the cherry on top! Thank you for your love and encouragement and for always agreeing to "take a bite!"

Kathy's family: David, Laura, and Amanda, I cannot imagine life without you, and I love you all more than words can express. Thank you for everything!

What a bright and sunny day it was when our agent, Lisa Ekus, introduced us to BJ Berti, our senior editor at St. Martin's Press. It has been a delightful relationship since day one, and we continue to respect her knowledge, creativity, and unparalleled experience. We are grateful for the entire St. Martin's team and appreciate all they do to create such beautiful cookbooks.

We are grateful to work with The Lisa Ekus Group. Lisa Ekus, Sally Ekus, and every single member of the team are incredible, and we cannot thank them enough. Their expertise, guidance, and attention to detail are unequaled.

Delicious photographs by Staci Valentine add so much to this cookbook, and we are grateful for her talent. Thank you, Staci, and food stylist Alyse Sakai, for your artistic skills and hard work.

There are so many more friends and colleagues who reach out and help us on our journey, and we want to thank each of you.

And most important, thank you to our friends online, who taste our recipes in their own kitchens and serve them at their own dinner tables. Please continue to journey with us at **www.pluggedintocooking.com**.

Index